Could I Really Be Autistic?

of related interest:

Women and Girls on the Autism Spectrum, Second Edition
Understanding Life Experiences from Early Childhood to Old Age
Sarah Hendrickx
Foreword by Judith Gould
ISBN 978 1 80501 069 2
eISBN 978 1 80501 070 8

Thumbsucker
An Illustrated Journey Through an Undiagnosed Autistic Childhood
Eliza Fricker
ISBN 978 1 83997 854 8
eISBN 978 1 83997 855 5

Stories of Autistic Joy
Laura Kate Dale
ISBN 978 1 83997 809 8
eISBN 978 1 83997 810 4

Autism and Masking
How and Why People Do It, and the Impact It Can Have
Dr Felicity Sedgewick, Dr Laura Hull & Helen Ellis
ISBN 978 1 78775 579 6
eISBN 978 1 78775 580 2

Rediscovered
A Compassionate and Courageous Guide for Late
Discovered Autistic Women (and Their Allies)
Catherine Asta
ISBN 978 1 80501 150 7
eISBN 978 1 80501 151 4

COULD I REALLY BE AUTISTIC?

Sarah and Jess Hendrickx

FOREWORD BY TONY ATTWOOD

Jessica Kingsley Publishers
London and Philadelphia

First published in Great Britain in 2026 by Jessica Kingsley Publishers
An imprint of John Murray Press

1

Copyright © Sarah Hendrickx and Jess Hendrickx 2026

Foreword Copyright © Tony Attwood 2026

This book contains mention of abuse, alcohol, anxiety, drugs, eating disorder, trauma.

A CIP catalogue record for this title is available from the
British Library and the Library of Congress

ISBN 978 1 80501 343 3
eISBN 978 1 80501 344 0

Printed and bound in Great Britain by Clays Ltd.

Jessica Kingsley Publishers' policy is to use papers that are natural,
renewable and recyclable products and made from wood grown in
sustainable forests. The logging and manufacturing processes are expected
to conform to the environmental regulations of the country of origin.

Jessica Kingsley Publishers
Carmelite House
50 Victoria Embankment
London EC4Y 0DZ

www.jkp.com

John Murray Press
Part of Hodder & Stoughton Ltd
An Hachette Company

The authorized representative in the EEA is Hachette Ireland, 8 Castlecourt
Centre, Dublin 15, D15 XTP3, Ireland (email: info@hbgi.ie)

Contents

Foreword

I began my interest in autism as a psychology student in the early 1970s. At that time, a diagnosis of autism was usually confirmed in the preschool years based on significant developmental delay in language, play, intellect, behaviour, and social engagement. It was considered rare, supposedly occurring in 1 in 2,500 children. I have explored autism as an objective observer for over 50 years, but recently, self-recognition of autism has begun to occur in adults more widely through subjective self-exploration, with the question, *could I really be autistic?*

We now recognize that autism is expressed in many ways, with a range of abilities and adaptations. Most autistic individuals have fluent speech, imaginative play in childhood, and intellectual abilities in the normal range. They can consciously suppress and camouflage autistic behaviours, creating an interpersonal 'mask', have effective compensation strategies such as a career where the characteristics of autism are an advantage, and experience long-term relationships. However, they are nonetheless autistic according to our evolving understanding of autism.

Autism has always been a part of being human. Historically, we had a broader conceptualization of individual differences, and an autistic person may have been considered eccentric but valued in their contribution to society or supported by their family. If they had what we now describe as autistic burnout they would have been admitted to a psychiatric institution with a diagnosis of atypical schizophrenia. When I was a clinician in a large psychiatric institution in London in the 1970s, I saw many patients who I would now consider autistic. Fortunately, today, we do not consider autism an expression of psychosis.

A recent development in our understanding of autism is that it often co-occurs with other medical and developmental conditions, as described by Sarah and Jess Hendrickx. These conditions, especially anxiety and ADHD, can have a more significant impact on daily life than autism. However, treatment and therapy for an additional condition will need to accommodate the characteristics of autism and the person's developmental history, which can include peer rejection, trauma, and low self-esteem. A diagnosis of autism can increase the effectiveness of psychological therapy and medical treatment.

When I complete a diagnostic assessment of an adult, I often say to the autistic person, 'Today, we discovered your autism. That discovery will provide a "lens" through which you can see your past, understanding for example why you were rejected and bullied by peers as a child, are extremely sensitive to specific sensory experiences, have difficulty coping with change and surprises, and making and keeping friends. The discovery will also help you make wise and informed decisions regarding current or future career choices and relationships, and have a more positive self-perception and less self-criticism.'

There is also the advantage of connecting with other autistic adults for guidance and support by reading autobiographies and becoming a member of an internet support group and seeking information on autism from social media.

We also recognize that autism can occur within and between generations in a family. Confirmation of being autistic can be of value in the person's family for greater understanding, compassion, and advice for other autistic family members, and being a mentor for autistic children and adults. Confirmation of autism can also lead to appropriate adjustments at work and potentially less stress and risk of autistic burnout.

If you think you may be autistic, this book will help clarify your thoughts and understanding of the range of expressions of autism and could transform your life and those who support you.

Professor Tony Attwood
Clinical Psychologist

Acknowledgements

Great thanks and appreciation to the legend that is Dr Linda Buchan, captain of the diagnostic ship that is Axia-ASD, for her clinical expertise.

Thanks also to the fabulous and multi-talented Jane Hill for her lengthy and detailed feedback on the first draft, and to Amy Lankester-Owen at JKP for her patience, guidance, and faith.

Introduction

If you have come across the concept of autism brought up in relation to yourself and thought 'I can't be autistic... can I?', then this book is for you. Perhaps a child in your family has been diagnosed as autistic, your therapist has suggested it, or people you know have called you 'Rain Man' throughout your life. Whatever the reason, here you are, with this book in your hands either seeking to confirm or dispel the idea that you might be autistic. We shall take you on a journey through autism diagnosis, and perhaps show you that the reasons that you thought you couldn't be autistic might just mean that you are...

Not so long ago, autism was considered to be rare, and this was certainly the belief of Leo Kanner, one of the pioneers of the modern day understanding of autism, who began working in the 1940s. At this time, and for several decades afterwards, it would have been unusual for anyone to have personally known an autistic person since diagnosis was not widely available and was largely limited to those who had significant intellectual disabilities and were male. Until recently our only templates for autistic people were those that we saw in the media, usually with 'savant' profiles. These are individuals with extraordinary abilities but also significant challenges, such as the lead character in the film *Rain Man*, Raymond Babbitt. Raymond was said to have been inspired by Kim Peek, an autistic man who could read two books at once and had the most incredible memory. Artist Stephen Wiltshire is another autistic savant who has a wonderful talent for replicating landscapes and buildings after only seeing them once. Then in 1995, neurologist and author Oliver Sacks introduced us to the unique and brilliant mind of Temple Grandin in his book *An Anthropologist on Mars* (1995). It is not surprising then, that most people did not identify themselves with these individuals due to their extreme profiles of both brilliance and challenge, and therefore did not see themselves as potentially autistic, because that's what we thought autism looked like.

In the last couple of decades things have changed; the internet and social media in particular have provided not only an accessible knowledge base of information about a plethora of conditions and experiences, but also a platform for sharing the voices and experiences of autistic people. The media of film, TV, radio, and print have increasingly featured autistic people – both celebrities and otherwise – and normalized their presence in everyday life. And this has not only led to a greater awareness of the existence of autistic people, but also a greater understanding of the breadth of autistic profiles and presentation. It is now not only savant autistics that grace our screens, but people who look and seem more like 'us' and who therefore are more easy for us to identify with. Social media in particular has led, in recent years, to a huge outpouring of information and experience sharing about autism, which has had both positive and less positive effects. On the one hand, the establishment of an accessible online autistic community has no doubt been literally life-saving to some autistic people who would previously have remained entirely alone and unaware of who they are, and, as a result of this isolation, suffered greatly with their mental health. On the other hand, social media has given a wide-reaching platform to those whose knowledge of what clinically constitutes autism is limited, and who may attribute characteristics as autistic which do not feature in the diagnostic criteria, and therefore would not be considered relevant in a diagnostic assessment. These people, although undoubtedly well-meaning, are not always helpful for those who are wading through the mire of information and trying to work out what exactly autism is, and whether it applies to them. This book attempts to clear up any misunderstandings and confusion by laying out as definitively as we can what is and what is not autism from a formal diagnostic perspective, whether it might apply to you, and what to do next.

What brings you here to wonder whether you may be autistic? Could it be that a friend or family member has been diagnosed? Perhaps you have read or seen something about an autistic person's experience that resonated with you? It is possible that you have felt different in some intangible way for much of your life. Perhaps you have been described as 'weird' or 'odd' by others and struggle with various aspects of everyday life – work, relationships, health – that others seem to find effortless. You may have tried several different therapists or read many self-development books to get to the bottom of this, but found that, whilst helpful with some aspects of your life, you have never quite found the root cause, and therefore the solution.

You may well have developed one or more narratives throughout your life to explain all or some of the above experiences, which likely began in childhood, determining that it's because you were shy, tall, short, clever, Black, gay, new at the school, foreign, an only child, from a large family, or an abusive family, too posh, too poor, deaf, blind, fat, moved around a lot, and so on...

If any of the above sounds familiar: welcome, you are not alone. These questions and thoughts are typical of adults who have come across the concept of autism in relation to themselves, which has facilitated a new and broader understanding of how autism may present: that it's not only nerdy boys with an encyclopaedic knowledge of dinosaurs (but there are plenty of those too), and that maybe it could be an explanation that fits.

This first encounter with autism in relation to oneself often evokes curiosity, followed by further research. As the investigation continues, the list of apparently disparate symptoms, characteristics, and challenges that the person has faced may all be brought together under the explanatory umbrella of autism. There can be tears and amazement that the descriptions of the lived experiences of autism match so closely with their own – 'that's my life. It's like that person is inside my head'. There is often a shock; a light bulb moment, sometimes swiftly followed by doubt. How can I be autistic? Surely someone would have spotted it by now? I'm too old/clever/social/married etc. but that niggling, nagging curiosity never quite goes away. Diagnosis feels like too big a step. What if I am wrong; I may look foolish? It costs a lot of money, or, in the case of state health service funded options, I may be taking an appointment from someone who really needs it. What difference will a diagnosis at this stage in my life make anyway? We've seen and heard it all before and we hope that we can help.

This book is your pathway towards answering some or all of the above questions and guiding you towards deciding whether you could really be autistic. Once you have come to some point of clarity on this initial question, we offer some options of possible steps you may want to take following that in terms of diagnosis, self-diagnosis, or further support.

Our experience in carrying out more than 1500 autism assessments between us has allowed us to gather a wealth of knowledge, not only of the diagnostic assessment process (which we have covered as best we can, since countries, cultures, healthcare systems and diagnostic providers vary), but also in hearing the same stories repeatedly about how individuals came across the idea of autism, why it feels relevant to them and why they think they might be autistic (or can't possibly be autistic). We see patterns of common journeys towards autism as an explanation for their differences and challenges, common associated factors and common questions and misconceptions about what autism truly looks like. All of this is presented in this book as a series of definitions, explanations, resources, and questions for the reader to digest and reflect upon to enable them to consider whether there is a real likelihood that they may be autistic or whether another explanation fits better. This process will also facilitate the gathering of relevant evidence (or lack of it) should a diagnostic assessment be worthy of consideration, taking the reader through the diagnostic criteria and outlining the nature and significance of examples which may be requested and required for clinical diagnostic assessment. Throughout the book you will have opportunities to reflect upon and give yourself a score on how your thoughts about being autistic are increasing or decreasing, and collate these scores in Chapter 8, Decision Time, to assist in making the decision whether self-diagnosis, formal assessment, or some other path is the best one for you right now. At the end in the Resources section, we have also provided resources for autism organizations around the world, and information on every other associated or alternative condition that we have mentioned along with recommendations for books and other resources to check out.

Once we have got all of the 'Am I? Aren't I?' information-gathering stuff out of the way, we present ideas and approaches for the 'what happens now?' part of possible diagnosis: the point where you have either received an autism positive outcome, made a conclusive self-diagnosis, or not, and are wondering what to do next. The diagnosis is the start of the journey, not the end, and afterwards comes the emotional processing of the outcome, which can take some time and may at points feel like a rollercoaster of conflicting emotions. We discuss thoughts on this along with considerations about disclosure – who to and when – along with finding support and a community that meets the needs of your new autistic identity, or moving on from the idea of autism entirely if it doesn't fit, or if another explanation fits better instead.

We hope that this book will pique your curiosity at least; you likely wouldn't have bought it unless you had some suspicion of your potential autistic nature. If someone else bought you this book: they are trying to tell you something, and that something is that they suspect you may be autistic. Maybe give it a look, even if it's just to prove them wrong. You never know, it just might change your life.

For Information

This book is not a diagnostic tool. It does not constitute, support, replace, or guarantee any diagnostic outcome of an autism clinical diagnosis. Despite the DSM-5 and ICD-11 diagnostic criteria being universally used around the world, the application of the criteria and the ethos, knowledge, and experience of the diagnostician will vary widely and therefore the outcome for one person in one diagnostic setting may be different if they had been seen by a different diagnostician. You may feel that you very clearly meet the diagnostic criteria, but the diagnostician that you see may have a different opinion.

Our aim is to assist in the collection of potentially suitable evidence should you decide to seek a clinical assessment, in the hope that you can give yourself the best chance of an accurate outcome. You should carry out your own due diligence in selecting an appropriate diagnostician – should you be fortunate enough to have a choice.

There are many opinions about the diagnostic set of criteria itself and its ability to accurately define a person as autistic, whether it is too narrow, or even too broad. For the sake of clinical integrity, this book uses the DSM-5 and ICD-11 criteria as its baseline because these are the baseline for clinical diagnosis anywhere and everywhere in the world. We do not believe that we can simply ignore or adjust them to meet our own opinions or agendas, and have not done so. These criteria may be less important if only self-diagnosis is sought, since one will not be subjected to the application of them in a clinical setting, but for those who seek formal diagnostic assessment, it is useful to know what they are and what is generally required to meet them.

Autism diagnosis is subjective as there is currently no genetic or definitive test to determine its presence. The level of understanding and acceptance of the adult autistic experience varies from country to country for many reasons including education, culture, language and economics, but it would be fair to say that in general, the Anglophone world generates the largest number of research papers and autistic-led content on social media, therefore supporting a broader definition of autism than some other countries and cultures.

The autistic community is broad in terms of intellectual level, ranging from individuals with severe learning disabilities to those with very high intellectual abilities (both typically defined by IQ level). It is our expectation that those consulting this book for their own or their loved ones' deliberation are more likely to not be facing any significant intellectual challenges, such as having a low IQ score, else they might find this book inaccessible. Whilst an individual with learning disabilities may well be autistic, and the autistic character- istics featured in this book will apply to them, it may be harder to identify and assess. This could be due to the person having, for exam- ple, a non-verbal communication profile, which may make it harder for them to share their thoughts and emotions, or challenges with insight, thereby not necessarily experiencing the sense of 'difference' that many potentially autistic people feel. It may also be the case that due to possible developmental delays and high support needs among this population, they are already under the care of professionals who can assess them, reducing the need for the type of information pro- vided in this book. Therefore, whilst this book may have some use for those of this profile, they are not the primary audience and their needs have not been fully covered.

As UK authors and diagnosticians, our perspective is naturally derived from our experiences of the UK-based view of autism, which may not be the same elsewhere. In terms of pathways towards diag- nosis, these again vary from country to country and we have tried not to be too UK-centric in this. The tools used in diagnosis will be different in other places, and we have outlined the main clinical processes, but cannot know them all. For the most part, we have assumed that, for many adults reading this book, privately funded diagnosis may be the quickest and easiest to access option (aside from the significant cost) since state health service funded diagnosis at best involves a lengthy wait, or at worst – as is the case in many countries – is non-existent. For those in the UK, the state-funded Right to Choose scheme is currently likely to be the best option for the fastest funded route to an NHS diagnosis. This scheme allows you to choose the provider who carries out your autism (or other neurodevelopmental diagnosis), regardless of your home location. As many diagnoses are carried out online these days, this can facilitate the choice of a recommended assessment provider. Facebook groups, Threads, and Reddit forums can be a useful place to ask people where they have had positive adult diagnostic experiences.

In taking the matter of seeking diagnosis forward in your own country and circumstances, you are on your own, as this is beyond the remit of this book. We present the notion of self-diagnosis as a potentially viable option either temporarily or permanently, should external assessment be unnecessary or unavailable.

We have used the term 'neurotypical' or 'non-autistic' to define a person with a typical developmental or non-autistic profile, and the term 'neurodivergent' to describe someone who has one or more neurodevelopmental conditions, such as autism, ADHD, dyslexia, or dyspraxia.

Your Authors

Sarah Hendrickx is a seven-times author of books on autism and neurodiversity, including the bestselling *Women and Girls on the Autism Spectrum*, 2nd edition (2024); the 1st edition of which sold 45,000+ copies. She was late-diagnosed as autistic and has combined type ADHD. For the past 14 years, Sarah has carried out more than 1200 non-clinical and clinical diagnostic assessments as an independent practitioner, for the Defence Science and Technology Laboratory (DSTL) which is an executive agency of the UK's Ministry of Defence, and for Axia-ASD, a UK-based diagnostic service provider delivering National Health Service (NHS) and self-funded private diagnoses. As well as working as an autism assessor, she has taken part in the development of training materials for the UK Department of Education funded National Autism Training Programme, Scottish Autism's Right Click Programme for autistic women and girls, and The National Autistic Society's professional module for clinicians diagnosing women and girls. Sarah has also delivered more than 1000 training and keynote conference presentations across the world. She has a Postgraduate Certificate in Asperger syndrome and a Master's degree in Autism, and spent many years as a project manager for an autism mentoring project as well as working in educational support and residential care. Sarah also has an autistic partner, two autistic children, and many other family members both diagnosed and in denial.

Jess Hendrickx is a published author, contributing a chapter on autism and eating to Sarah Hendrickx's second edition of her book *Women and Girls on the Autism Spectrum*. Jess first started her career in the autism field as a mentor, supporting autistic individuals both pre- and post-diagnosis. During this time, she helped many individuals to come to terms with what autism meant for them. Jess now runs a private company, Hendrickx Associates, conducting private non-clinical autism and ADHD assessments, as well as clinically supervised NHS and privately funded autistic and ADHD diagnosis in partnership with Axia-ASD. Alongside Jess' work as a diagnostician, she delivers training to both private and public sector clients, working with corporate companies, the NHS, and the Ministry of Justice, as well as speaking at international conferences. Jess was diagnosed as dyslexic when she was 16 years old, and autistic and combined type ADHD in her 30s.

How to Use This Book

You can, of course, use it any way you like, but here's one idea.

At the end of Chapters 2–7 of the book, you will find a section for your own notes, some questions for you to answer and the opportunity to give yourself a score from 0–10 on the likelihood of being autistic from the information gathered in that chapter. A score of 0 would mean that you have no confidence at all in being diagnosed as autistic and 10 meaning that you have very high confidence of receiving such a diagnosis, should you choose to undertake one. Most likely you will be somewhere in between. You can also make notes on why you have given yourself this score and what factors stopped it from being higher or lower, e.g., listing examples of how your profile and experiences aligned with what you read, and examples of how they didn't.

Chapter 8 is Decision Time, where you can collate all of your notes and end-of-chapter scores from the preceding chapters and summarize at that point, having read all the information, how high your overall confidence of being autistic is and what you may decide to do next. If you score 10/10 in all of the chapters, we are afraid to say that there is no prize for coming top. Only the knowledge that you have a high chance of being autistic (which should be reward enough!). Congratulations if this is you. Papers will be checked for cheating.

If you do decide to move towards formal assessment, these notes will assist you in completing an autism assessment questionnaire, which you will very likely be asked to complete for any autism assessment. You may need to transfer the information onto any form that you are given by the assessment service provider, as they may want it in their own format, but you will have done a lot of the work in gathering evidence of how you meet the diagnostic criteria.

So, with all the admin and explanations out of the way, let's commence our quest to find out if you could really be autistic, or not.

Chapter 1

What Exactly Is Autism?

Understanding the Diagnostic Criteria

Warning: The next few pages are heavy reading and can be skipped if detailed, academic descriptions of diagnostic criteria are not your thing. You can join us again at the start of Chapter 2 where we will explain the diagnostic criteria using real-world examples, rather than academic jargon. We have included this current chapter for those people who like to know everything and ask 'why?' a lot.

In order to begin our journey into the world of autism diagnosis and how this might apply to you, it is useful to understand what exactly constitutes autism from a clinical perspective. We shall explain the official diagnostic criteria. We won't get involved in debates about the accuracy of the criteria in identifying autism, but will stick with them as they are, since this is what is currently required for a formal clinical diagnosis.

The generally accepted diagnostic criteria for autism spectrum disorder (ASD) – to give the condition its official diagnostic name, although many people prefer the less negative sounding autism spectrum condition – feature in two different diagnostic manuals developed by two different organizations. These manuals are reviewed and updated periodically to consider new research and thinking about many different conditions, and thus each has a version number which changes following these updates.

One was established by the American Psychiatric Association (APA) and is called the Diagnostic and Statistical Manual of Mental Disorders (DSM). Version five is the most current and this is typically referred to as the DSM-5, which was released in 2013, with version six likely to appear some time before 2028 based on previous patterns of revisions. There has been a text revision to this version (but not a new version), which is referred to as the DSM-5-TR (text revised). The other manual is from the World Health Organization and is called the International Classification of Diseases (ICD); version 11 is the most current (typically referred to as the ICD-11), having been released in 2022, with no date currently known for the next edition. There may be national variance in the release of these editions and some individual countries may still be working with earlier editions rather than the latest ones. The presence of the two diagnostic systems is worth mentioning because they each have reasonably clear worldwide geographic boundaries within which they are applied, which means that the criteria that you may be measured on will differ depending on where you live. Whilst they are broadly similar (more on that later), there may be some differences in their application, as the ICD-11 criteria appear to be a little broader in scope than the DSM criteria. In general terms, the DSM criteria are favoured by the USA and the ICD criteria by the rest of the world – the UK and Europe in particular.

The process of an autism diagnostic assessment will have at its core these diagnostic criteria, but it may be administered in a variety of different ways, using clinical tools, questionnaires, tests, and interviews, many of which will be discussed later on in the book.

In summary, the criteria for an autism diagnosis require evidence of significant lifelong atypicality from standard developmental and behavioural norms in the areas of social functioning and flexibility. The manifestation of these broad terms is wide and varied, but there must be evidence of these core differences. Don't panic, all will be clearly explained.

Let's look at what the diagnostic criteria require a person to present or demonstrate in order to meet the diagnostic threshold. We will start with an overview of the types of items listed in the criteria, and follow that with some real-life examples of how a person might be seen to meet these criteria. You can begin to make some notes in the section at the end of the book of anything that resonates. Something important to note before we go any further is that autism is fundamentally a neurodevelopmental condition, which affects the way that autistic people process and interact with every aspect of their physical and social environment. The result of these neurological (brain) differences is that autistic people may make sense of things differently, which leads to them behaving differently.

Thus, despite the diagnostic criteria being rooted in behavioural items; autism is actually based in perception and processing differences, which may result in those behaviours. As we will learn, some of the 'autistic' behaviours may stem from another cause and some may be hidden due to learned masking strategies, which a person may adopt after learning from experience that their natural ways of being may not be deemed acceptable for the society that they live in. Therefore, autism exists in the 'why' of any 'autistic' behaviour that is present or any typical behaviour that is absent, rather than in the behaviour itself. For example, there may be many reasons that a person doesn't have many friends, and autism is only one of those. Reflecting on 'why' you do or don't do any of the autistic features that you identify with will give the true insight into whether autism is a good explanation for you and your experiences. Another example of where careful questioning and reflection is necessary is when a person coming for assessment says that they must go to the gym every night of the week and that not doing so causes them distress. On first glance, this may appear to be a possibly autistic behaviour relating to routine, repetition, and sameness, and a discomfort with changes of plan. When asking the person 'why?' they feel distressed by missing going to the gym each night, they say that if they don't take part in physical activity every day they feel like they are 'climbing the walls'. They go on to describe how the activity and movement makes them feel 'even and balanced'. Now, with this additional information, the feature of maintaining a routine of going to the gym starts to look more like a possible ADHD trait (movement, variety). It could certainly be the case that the person has both autism and ADHD, and it could certainly be the case that exercise helps them manage stress and anxiety as an autistic person. What is important here is that we do not take the surface level 'Yes' response to a question such as 'Do you stick rigidly to routines?' as the full picture.

Social Communication and Social Interaction
These items are required to be present in multiple settings (home, school, work, daily life) and throughout the lifespan (childhood and adulthood). Both the DSM-5 and ICD-11 requirements for this section are extremely similar and, for our purposes, do not require individual consideration – if you meet the criteria for one, you will meet it for the other.

Social Reciprocity
This is the skill of turn-taking, sharing of interests and emotions, initiation, and response to social input.

Non-Verbal Social Behaviours
This includes the using, reading, interpretation of, and response to facial expressions, eye contact, and body language/gestures. It refers to both your own usage of such behaviours, and your ability to identify and respond typically to those same behaviours in others.

Developing, Understanding, and Sustaining Relationships
This covers sharing play in childhood, adapting behaviour to different social contexts – recognizing social hierarchies, for example – and having an interest in establishing relationships, and making and keeping friends.

Restricted, Repetitive, and/or Inflexible Interests, Patterns of Behaviour, and Activities

There is a slight difference in the specification between the DSM-5 and ICD-11 for this section, which is worth a mention for clarity, but is unlikely to make much difference to the diagnostic outcome.

The DSM-5 requires two out the following four subcategories to be met:

Repetitive Speech, Use of Objects or Movements

This item describes the performing of repetitive physical movements such as rocking, spinning, or the rhythmic tapping of fingers, strong attachment to certain objects and also repeated words or phrases such as copied or prepared scripts to aid interaction.

Requirement for Routines, Sameness, Inflexible Thought Patterns, and Behaviours

This item includes a strong preference for all aspects of daily living to remain certain, expected, and familiar with any deviation from this causing distress or avoidance.

Intense and Fixed Interests

This element requires the presence of one or more singular interests that are unusual in their depth and intensity. The topics can be anything, but there is an all-encompassing nature to them which leads the individual to repetitively think and talk about, and engage with, the interest. This may lead to an expert level of knowledge being attained.

Atypical Sensory Profile

Evidence is required of hypo (low) sensitivity or hyper (high) sensitivity to one or more senses – light, sound, smell, taste, touch, movement, proprioception (sensing the position and placement of your own body), and interoception (internal signals). The presentation of sensory differences typically involves avoidance or seeking of one or more of the specific sensory stimuli, as listed above.

Qualifiers for the DSM-5-TR and ICD-11

The ICD-11 differs from the DSM-5 by not making any specific number of individual features a requirement, but describes very similar requirements in terms of meeting the criteria. The focus of the ICD-11, as in the DSM-5, is on lack of adaptability to change, social contexts and circumstances, adherence to rules, intense interests, repetitive behaviours, and an atypical sensory profile.

Both sets of diagnostic criteria have similar general thresholds that need to be met across all of the individual diagnostic elements required in order for diagnosis to be given. The first of these threshold specifiers requires evidence of 'persistent deficits' (APA, 2013; WHO, 2022). What this means is that when compared to a peer of the same age and same developmental level, an autistic person will have more challenges, most of the time. We can debate the concept of 'deficits' and 'challenges', and may prefer the term 'differences', but this is how the criteria phrase it. The characteristics featured are all defined as a comparison against what is determined to be typical development, cognition, or behaviour. 'Persistent' indicates that these differences are seen throughout the lifespan and are not the result of trauma, illness, or other short-lived circumstances. Both sets of criteria offer qualifiers here which state that the characteristics must be present from infancy; they may not fully show themselves or cause challenges until 'social demand exceeds limited capacity' (APA, 2013), or they may be 'masked by learned strategies in later life' (APA, 2013). What this means is that when younger, and in the care of family, finding reading people's faces difficult, lining up your cars, or finding going to new places very distressing may present less of an issue than when you are required to live an independent adult life. The masking aspect results from where autistic people have observed and learned that their innate way of engaging with the world doesn't serve them well due to negative feedback from others, and they then consciously try to learn how to emulate the norms of those around them to ease their passage through a complicated world that seems to make little sense. More on this in a while.

The second threshold specifier concerns the level of impairment to functioning that these characteristics impose. It is necessary for them to cause significant challenges in a range of areas, including social, educational, employment, and personal aspects of life when compared to a same age peer. The individual themselves may not feel 'impaired' and may have used their autistic differences as a strength, but this is how the diagnostic criteria measure this difference. We shall look at these in more detail as we progress and try to identify what exactly constitutes 'significant impairment', although this is one of the likely key areas of varying opinion (and therefore potential diagnostic outcome) of different diagnosticians.

The DSM-5 diagnostic measure also identifies a severity level ranging from 3–1 in terms of a decreasing level of support required. This does not equate to intellectual level, as it may be that a person with no intellectual disability and an average or above average level of IQ may require very substantial support due to the impact of being autistic in a non-autistic world. Intelligence does not necessarily mean that a 'milder' or 'high-functioning' autistic experience is a given, and these terms are unhelpful and do not indicate the full picture of an autistic person's profile.

Cultural Considerations

There is a cultural aspect that is important to note here. For example, if a person originates from a culture where making no eye contact is typical of the general population and/or socially expected, and then relocates to somewhere where eye contact is culturally typical, then this element of the criteria would not be met despite the person's behaviour indicating a 'deficit' in eye contact in their new culture. In terms of diagnosis, cultural differences are very important. When assessing individuals from other countries and cultures in the UK, it is necessary to determine whether they were considered atypical in their culture of origin (throughout their lifespan there), and not just in their new culture.

Chapter 2

Diagnostic Features of Autism in the Real World

Welcome back to those who skipped the academic bit above. Things should be much easier to digest from here on in.

So, now we have it clear that whatever potential autism-defined features you experience must have always been there (although perhaps hidden, or not very troublesome), and that they must cause some sort of significant difference to your life when compared to your peers. From here we move on to what exactly constitutes the package of autism defined by the DSM and ICD criteria in more detail, as it perhaps feels a bit vague right now. We have in this chapter given real-life examples of how each required element of the criteria presents in both stereotypical and non-stereotypical ways. The section headings may not exactly match those in the diagnostic criteria as we have broken them down further to aid understanding and clarity. These examples are by no means universal, meaning that they do not apply to every single autistic person on the planet, but are given to illustrate possible motivations or reactions. Use them as a guide only and consider how you respond to the situations provided, along with any others that you have come across throughout your life and reacted to in an atypical way. It is important to emphasize, however, that all required elements of the diagnostic criteria must be met, not just one or two. If this is the case for you, then you may find a better explanation within Chapter 6, What Else Could It Be?, which outlines similarities and differences between autism and other conditions.

As we have previously mentioned, it might be useful for you to take notes on what resonates with you as you read, especially in this chapter as there is a lot of information and real-life examples given. You will then have all the information to hand when you reach the end of the chapter and complete the self-assessment checklist.

Communication

Autistic people can be very effective communicators, as is evidenced in the number of autistic authors and academics. However, the skills that may be intuitive to neurotypical people tend to be learned and honed throughout autistic people's lives. When we assess people, we are looking for differences in verbal and non-verbal communication, across different settings which include home, work/education, and social. These communication differences refer to small talk/social chit chat skills and desire, ability to read and interpret non-verbal cues (facial expressions, body language, tone of voice, and jokes/sarcasm), importance of precise language, preference for direct language, and any other individual preferences for communicating.

Many autistic people feel they need to mask their differences in order to fit into society. Every person masks to a certain extent, regardless of neurotype (during job interviews for example), but the frequency and intensity with which autistic people do it tends to have a detrimental effect on them and can be very draining. Masking in terms of communication may include copying accents, laughing along with a joke even if you haven't understood it, stopping yourself from being blunt, repeating phrases that you have heard other's use, and mimicking people's body language, facial expressions, and tone of voice. When you change how you communicate this also masks the difficulties you may be having, and some people are more successful at this than others. This can lead to confusion when others learn of the effort it takes to appear 'normal'. They will not see the metaphorical cogs turning in your head or be able to hear the constant inner-monologue (or internal chatter) that monitors your social performance in the hope of avoiding doing something that may be perceived as socially awkward or unacceptable (sometimes termed as a 'faux pas' in diagnostic jargon), and being seen as weird.

When considering your own communication differences, it is important that you do not compare yourself to people from other countries and cultures. Every country and culture's benchmark for developmental milestones and what is considered socially acceptable is likely to be different, so it is vital that you are comparing yourself to people who speak the same language and are from the same country/culture as you.

Communication Differences in Childhood

To be autistic you do not have to have delayed speech or be non-speaking, but your differences in communication do need to be evident from childhood. Some parents of autistic children report that their child started speaking much earlier than is typical (in English-speaking countries, the developmental milestone for communication is speaking in 2–3 word sentences at approximately 2 years of age). Parents also report that the amount autistic children talk may differ to the child's non-autistic peers. They may be very chatty and happy to talk to anyone about anything, whilst others may prefer not to speak, possibly due to feeling anxious or having no interest in the conversation. It is not uncommon for autistic children to have an idiosyncratic speech pattern and develop an adult style of speech at a young age. Some people report that as a child they would sound very formal, use advanced vocabulary, want to speak about topics not stereotypically associated with children (i.e., history, mechanics, politics etc.) and because of this preferred the company of adults rather than their peers. Many autistic children see no reason not to alert adults to errors even if those adults are teachers or others in authority (some autistic adults continue to do this, which can cause issues in the workplace), and can be confused when they are reprimanded for being rude when they were just trying to be helpful. In Western societies, correcting someone in authority is often deemed socially unacceptable, but the autistic child is likely to not understand this, or care, as righting the wrong is far more important. These adults may include teachers, parents, grandparents, other family members, and even complete strangers.

Some autistic children may not intuitively understand the expectation of turn-taking in conversations as their neurotypical peers do, which can lead to them both speaking over people or staying very quiet. This may be because they do not know how or when to enter the conversation. They also may not say hello or goodbye, ask questions about other people's lives, or want to engage with people they are not interested in or feel comfortable with. Others may be more comfortable in conversing with adults rather than their peers, and seek this out in school, at home, or when at friend's houses. The general consensus is that they feel less judged by adults, and, as previously mentioned, the topics of conversation tend to be more appealing.

Even if an autistic child can speak, there may be times in which they become situationally non-speaking (otherwise known as situational mutism), due to feeling uncomfortable, anxious, or overwhelmed. These people have the words but in those moments cannot communicate verbally, and may need to use gestures, or get a parent, sibling, or friend to speak for them. Other children may be completely non-speaking, and have to use signing or other means to communicate. It is important to remember that just because someone cannot speak does not mean that they cannot communicate at all, and for some non-speaking autistic people their speech will develop over time; for others they will be non-speaking for their entire lives.

At school, autistic children may feel very anxious at the prospect of raising their hand to ask or answer questions, read aloud, or give presentations. At a young age you may not be able to articulate why, but later in life autistic adults may reflect and feel it was because they were worried they might do something wrong and be laughed at. In social situations with their peers, autistic children may find it hard to enter the conversation and may prefer to be on the periphery and observe instead. The sensory aspect of being in groups can also have an impact on how comfortable someone is to communicate; if it is too noisy, it can be very hard to focus on the conversation, or keep up with multiple conversations happening at once. On the other end of the scale are the chatterboxes. These children can dominate conversation, interrupt people, change the subject, and fail to identify subtle social cues which indicate when someone wants them to stop speaking. They are likely to enjoy talking at great length about their interests and lives, and make comments about what they see which others may find rude or unusually honest.

How autistic children engage in play tends to differ to non-autistic children, especially with regard to how they communicate with their peers during games. They may become overwhelmed if the other child is not interacting with them in the way that they want or need, or goes against the rules the autistic child has devised. Some autistic children can come across as quite dominant in play and are not afraid to tell people off when they do something that they had not anticipated. However, others can be quite passive and not want to stand up to their peers, preferring to just follow what other people are doing. What appears to be less typical and more complicated for autistic children is mutual and reciprocal conversation and play. In general, autistic children are less likely to come up with dialogue between their toys, and prefer to set scenes with them rather than engaging in more imaginative play. When autistic children use communication in their play, it is more likely to be repeating dialogue that they have heard elsewhere – in real life or from films/programmes/books – rather than their own original narratives. A lot of autistic children love to read, and because of this have amazing vocabularies and knowledge about certain topics. The books may be fact based or fictional stories, with fiction giving them a world to escape into. They may also enjoy reading the same books over and over, or collecting and reading books in a series.

Some autistic children enjoy repeating sounds, words, and phrases over and over, which is a phenomenon called echolalia. The repetition of words and sounds is a normal part of speech development that normally stops around 3 years of age, however, in autistic people it can carry on into adulthood. Echolalia in autistic people can be both voluntary and involuntary, and is sometimes considered a form of stimming (self-soothing behaviour), as one of the motivations for repeating certain sounds and noises is that they feel or sound nice. The words or sounds could be repeated either straight after hearing them or at any time in the future, and the frequency at which they are repeated can range from just once to multiple times over a long period of time.

It is expected that how you communicate will change over time, especially as a lot of autistic people learn the rules and become very successful communicators in a neuronormative world. Communication styles not only change as you get older, but will also depend on the situation you are in, who you are with, and how much energy you have. You may have started off incredibly chatty, but after years of being told you are 'too much', your confidence is knocked and you become much more reserved. In contrast, you may have started life being much quieter or even non-speaking (situational or not), but if you have now found your voice there may be no silencing you.

General Social Communication in Adulthood

As mentioned previously, every autistic person is different – some are very chatty and some are not. In a one-to-one situation, with someone you feel comfortable and safe with, you may be very happy to have a reciprocal free-flowing conversation, especially if it's about something you are passionate or knowledgeable about. However, this can then change if you are forced to interact with a large group of people, and for some it doesn't matter if they know them or not, the anxiety will still be present. Regardless of which group dynamic you are in – work, education, or socially – all can provide their own unique set of problems, but a common theme across all settings is a difficulty not knowing how to enter a conversation. When you do not know when to speak this can lead to people speaking over others, waiting too long and the conversation moving on before having had a chance to speak, or feeling anxious that you may say the 'wrong' thing.

When you do not understand how much information is too much, it can lead to over-explaining and giving more detail than is considered necessary or wanted by the other person. This is especially true when talking about intense interests, where autistic people report a compulsion to speak and share *all* of their knowledge, compared to during more general chat, tending to keep quiet and just observe. It can be quite baffling if your conversational partner does not have quite the same enthusiasm for the minute particulars of your current intense interest. Being very knowledgeable about a certain topic can make autistic people fabulous public speakers and teachers, as they get to stand up and share their excitement and expertise with a room full of people, who are there for the sole purpose of listening to them. There may be a stark difference between this person on and off the stage, especially when they need to engage in small talk.

'Boring', 'pointless', 'awkward', 'superficial', 'hate it' – these are just a handful of the common answers people give when they are asked what their feelings are about engaging in small talk and social chit chat. As we get older, many of us learn how to mask our disinterest in this form of communication, but it doesn't mean it gets any easier or enjoyable. If you are nodding along in agreement, you have probably honed your small talk script, making sure to ask the socially accepted questions, force a smile, and try not to overshare or switch the topic of conversation back to yourself and your interests. You are probably also aware that when someone asks you how you are, most of the time, they do not actually want to know, but you may have learned that the hard way after years of answering honestly and oversharing your deepest, darkest inner thoughts. Not every autistic person hates small talk; for some it can be enjoyable as it gives them a time-limited and structured form of interaction in which they have learned the rules of what to say and not say, but in general, autistic people would much rather talk about their interests or have conversations on a much deeper level. One tool that some autistic people use to aid in conversing is scripting, rehearsing or having a bank of questions memorized, so that they do not need to think of what to say on the spot and feel as prepared as possible. These scripts provide a framework for starting and maintaining conversations, along with asking and answering questions. Many autistic people also use scripts when making phone calls, as it is often the case that autistic people do not enjoy making and receiving phone calls due to the unpredictable nature of not knowing who will pick up (or if they will pick up) or what will be asked of them. This along with having no visual cues can make phone calls anxiety inducing. It can be easier if there is a purpose to the phone call (making a doctor's appointment, ordering a takeaway) as they can prepare scripts in advance, but many still say that they put off making the call until the absolute last minute. Whether it is on the phone or in person, the only issue with scripting is if the other person says something unexpected or changes the subject, which will leave the autistic person feeling unprepared and potentially unsure what to say.

A 2021 study on autism and communication preferences concluded that for many autistic people written communication is the preferred method (Howard and Sedgewick, 2021, p. 2271). When communicating in writing, there is more processing time to assess what has been said, how to reply, and a response tends not to be expected straightaway. The original message can be revisited multiple times, therefore allowing them time to plan exactly what they need to say, and edit it before sending. When in person, you do not have the time to be able to be so measured, and your communication may also be impacted by the sensory environment. The other great thing about written communication is that if you've had enough of communicating you can just shut your laptop or switch off your phone and ignore people!

Bluntness, Perceived Social Errors, and Knowing What to Say When

There are so many rules around neuronormative communication, about what you can say, at what time, and to whom. There seem to be many topics that are off limits, such as not discussing serious, potentially volatile subjects like politics or religion with people you know have an opposing view, or discussing your bowel movements with a complete stranger. For some autistic people they may not understand or agree with these rules, feeling that openness and honesty is the best policy. Some autistic people tend to have a more blunt, direct, and honest communication style, which could include answering a question truthfully that non-autistic people would respond to with a lie (e.g., 'Do you like my outfit?') or pointing something out without thinking about the potential ramifications (e.g., loudly telling someone they have a huge pimple on their face). The majority of the time, there is no malicious intent, and there will likely be some level of shock, shame, or embarrassment when they find out they have inadvertently upset someone because of what they said. There may also be differences with how autistic people react to what they have been told, with this reaction not quite being what is expected. This may include a matter-of-fact remark or just staying silent due to having absolutely no idea what to say when, for example, being given news of someone's death.

It's important to add here that the idea of hierarchy can be confusing to some autistic people and they may struggle to abide by the social rules of someone being 'more senior' or in a position of authority. This can be seen across all age groups: in childhood it can present as arguing with parents and teachers, and in adulthood with bosses or even members of law enforcement. A common thought is that everyone is human and therefore should be interacted with in the same manner, regardless of social standing. It is not uncommon for autistic people to just communicate and treat people in the way they themselves want to be treated.

Precision, Clarity, and Accuracy of Language

Some autistic people describe themselves as pedantic due to their literal understanding of language and can find it difficult to understand communication when it is ambiguous, vague, or unclear, and may ask for clarification to a larger degree than most. For a lot of autistic people, it is very important that language is correct, so if an error is made by someone else, such as a mispronunciation, incorrect word, or misremembered information, it is very likely that it will have to be pointed out and questioned because this is necessary for comprehension. There are those who have learned that most people do not appreciate being corrected, so stop themselves from commenting, even though the error is very obvious to them.

When an autistic person is given instructions, it is likely that these will need to be very clear and concise, and may also be easier to follow if they are written down so that they can be referred back to. It can help if the instructions are broken down into individual steps, and given in the order of priority, so that all of the information is present and there is no need to fill in any missing information. When someone is vague it can lead to confusion and misunderstanding due to some autistic people being very literal and, for instance, only doing part of the task due to the verbal instructions given. An example of this is if an autistic person was told to do the laundry they may only put the clothes on to wash and not hang them up to dry as well, or if told they need a bath, responding with 'I can't, we only have a shower'. Many autistic people are likely to be able to work out the missing information, but it does take effort.

Non-Verbal Communication

When people communicate with each other they do not just use words to convey their message, but also different forms of non-verbal communication such as body language, facial expressions, and tone of voice to relay additional information on how they are feeling and what they are thinking. There are differences between autistic and non-autistic people in how these non-verbal cues are picked up, interpreted, and expressed. Many autistic people will be able to tell how someone is feeling or what they are thinking if their non-verbal cues are more obvious or exaggerated, such as crying or frowning, but may find it harder if they are more nuanced or neutral, such as tired or thinking. When someone is presenting in a more neutral way, this can be confusing as there is a lack of information being given, which may be misinterpreted as that person being upset with them. This in turn can cause the autistic person to ask, potentially repeatedly, what is wrong, and they may not believe it when someone says that they are fine. After a lifetime of learning how to read people, some autistic people end up being hypervigilant to the small changes in people's non-verbal cues but may not always understand exactly what that person is thinking or feeling, or how to react to it. Some people have developed a strategy where they have, in their own words, 'become a clown' and used humour to interact with people. These people have said that the only way that they can tell what mood someone is in or if the person likes them is if the person is laughing, and so they feel a sense of safety by provoking this response and knowing where they stand with that person.

With regards to expressing non-verbal cues, some autistic people may not do so in a stereotypical way and a lot of people say that their external presentation is not always matched by how they are feeling internally. Some autistic people have a particularly neutral face effect or do not emote in the same way as neurotypical people, which can lead to them being described as intense, serious, aloof, or stand-offish. This can lead some to make a conscious effort to smile even when they are feeling very anxious or uncomfortable, or to practise facial expressions in the mirror.

Many autistic people do not recognize when someone is being sarcastic or making a joke due to not noticing the tone of someone's voice, their facial expression, or the context of the comment which can lead to it being taken literally. It can be harder to decipher whether something was a sarcastic comment if it is delivered in a very deadpan way, or by someone they do not know as well. Even though it is fairly common for autistic people to not always pick up on sarcasm and jokes, they can use both sarcasm and humour in their own communication, often extremely well.

Social Relationships, Empathy, and Masking

The social relationships element of the diagnostic criteria is not just about how many friendships you have or if you have/haven't been in a romantic relationship, although these may be important factors of a bigger picture. To meet the criteria, autistic people have notable lifelong differences with their ability and desire to interact with others. This can include their capacity and motivations for socializing, engaging in intuitive eye contact, ability/desire to emotionally support others (empathizing), and how much/little masking of their autistic traits they engage in and why. Unsurprisingly, you can be autistic and have lots of friends and a successful and happy relationship with a partner, although quite commonly your friends and partners will be autistic or neurodivergent too.

Autistic people's motivations to socialize and have romantic relationships may differ from neurotypicals. Some autistic people find that it takes a lot of energy to make and maintain relationships, so are selective with who they spend their time with and energy on. Other autistic people have minimal interest in socializing altogether and are very happy spending their time alone. Then there are those who want and need a mixture of the two, which seems to be the most common.

When considering your own social life, think about the relationships you've had throughout your life – platonic and romantic – and if your desire/ability to be around people differs from that of your peers. Some cultures place a lot more importance on connections with people than others and it is important, once again, to take that into consideration.

Social Differences in Childhood

From a young age we start to form relationships and connections with other people. These tend to start with parents/caregivers, siblings, other family members and then people outside of our family network. For a lot of autistic people, their differences with socializing can be seen at a very young age. First signs may include not wanting to interact with people other than their parents/siblings, showing no interest in sharing toys or things they find interesting, and playing alongside their peers or adults instead of interacting directly with them. Their preferred activities may be solitary, or activity based, rather than imaginative play. As previously mentioned in the communication section, any imaginative or role play games are more likely to be based on real-life scenarios, copied from films, or led by other children. Active games and sports may help autistic children to engage with their peers as there are clearly defined rules and roles, which can make it easier to interact with others. This is also the case with extracurricular activities – they can enable autistic children to socialize, in a time managed and structured environment, around an activity that they really enjoy. However, they may not choose to socialize with their peers from these groups outside of these situations.

Once children start nursery school/kindergarten (around 2–3 years of age in most countries), these differences may become more noticeable as they spend extended periods of time outside of the family and in situations where there are more people. In these earlier years, autistic children may not have the same need to interact with their peers as neurotypical children. If an autistic child does want their peers to be involved in what they are playing, they may need them to follow their rules of the game and get upset when others do not do as they are told. This can lead to other children not wanting to play with the autistic child as they are considered too bossy, meaning that exclusion can start at a young age. Many autistic children would like friends but can struggle to make and maintain friendships. It can be tricky to initiate and then grow friendships if you do not know or understand the social rules around how much contact to make, or if you are unwilling to compromise and want everyone to do what you want. Some autistic children may be perceived as too intense as they focus all of their attention on one person and expect the same in return. On the other hand, others appear very passive or completely disinterested as they do not have the confidence to approach people, or may just go along with what others want to do so they can just fit in. Many people comment that they were quite confused as a child about why they were often left out of social groups and activities, which in turn left them feeling jealous of other children or lonely. In their mind, they were interacting and doing things in the same way as their peers, but did not seem to form the connections others had. It can be hard to navigate social group dynamics, and it may be that as a child you preferred to have one-to-one friendships if you found managing multiple people and their needs too overwhelming. For others, being in a group was easier as there was less pressure to speak and they could sit back and observe. What is often the case is that friendships made are often with children who are similar, as in they are also autistic, or are also an 'outsider' in some other way – racially or culturally different, shy, or having a disability, for example.

As we all remember, being a teenager is a confusing time, and if you then throw undiagnosed autism into the mix as well, navigating relationships throughout these years can be incredibly challenging.

43

For some they feel like they have been left behind by their peers once puberty hits, and their peers' interests move away from play and toys to romantic relationships, popular culture, and socializing all the time. This transition can appear to happen very quickly. During these years a lot of people find themselves on the periphery of social groups and feel like they do not fit in. This can be quite an isolating time, especially if you do not know that you are autistic and therefore why you keep 'getting it wrong'. For others they do their best to fit in and not to stand out for fear of being ostracized, and achieve this by copying their peers. This is when people start to mask or camouflage their autistic traits. There is a whole section on masking to come.

Attending large social events such as birthday parties, weddings and family parties can pose a challenge for autistic children, as they may not know what the neuronormative social expectations are and find the sensory aspect of them challenging. Large social events tend to be full of new people that you only meet for a brief period of time, so it's difficult to work out exactly how to interact with them. The unstructuredness of parties can also prove harder to navigate and a lot of people report that as a child they were happy to attend parties with a fixed activity (swimming, ice skating, soft play etc.) rather than discos or hang-outs. They may also have liked attending parties, not for the social aspect but because there was food or a bouncy castle. Sleepovers with friends either at other people's or their own homes can cause issues for different reasons. Some autistic people do not like having people in their space and touching their things, making it difficult when people stay over. When sleeping at a friend's house, there is a lack of normal routines and surroundings, along with needing to converse and socialize with unknown people (parents and siblings), all of which can lead to anxiety.

Unfortunately, many autistic people are bullied throughout childhood for being different, even if they do not have a diagnosis as a child. There are some people in the world that, even at a young age, can pick up on vulnerability and differences, and prey on this. Autistic children may not realize that someone is lying to them or has an ulterior motive, and when someone is trusting, they are unfortunately more likely to be taken advantage of. If you have been bullied at any point in your life, please remember that it was not your fault.

General Social Differences in Adulthood

Whether or not you have many, few, or no friends, if you are autistic, how you navigate relationships and your preference for them is likely to be different to neurotypical people. You may have a desire to have lots of friends, a few friends, or none. However, as was mentioned in the childhood section, making and maintaining relationships can continue to be difficult even as an adult. Your friendships may be initiated and led by others, and some autistic people feel that they do not know at what point someone becomes an actual or proper friend. Unfortunately, when you're an adult it's not as simple as saying 'Will you be my friend?' – this is likely to get some odd looks and comments, but it would be nice if it was that easy! Many autistic relationships are based on a shared interest, hobby, or activity, and there may be very little interest in socializing for the sake of it. Autistic people can end up compartmentalizing relationships and are not comfortable mixing people from one part of their life with another. To expand on this, people may feel that work colleagues should only be seen at work, that family is family, and friends are only seen to do the one activity they always do together. The idea of people from one aspect of their lives meeting others from a different part causes anxiety, and a common reason for the anxiety is that you may act differently with different people. Due to the toll social events can take, many autistic people will replay and ruminate on the events that have happened. If this is something that you do, it is likely to be negative, contemplating how people perceive you and what you did wrong. For some, this can disrupt sleep and they may think about things that have happened years before. This all adds to the narrative that as a potentially autistic person you are constantly 'getting it wrong' in regards to interacting with others.

Feelings around informal and large social events have been previously mentioned about childhood, but are still likely to pose difficulties in adulthood. Open-ended social events may cause more anxiety as you do not know exactly how long you will be around people or exactly what you'll be doing. Some autistic people like to take on a helping role at social events as it gives a purpose to their interactions with people. For example, if you are distributing the drinks at a party it can help to initiate conversations with less pressure, or if you busy yourself with the cooking or tidying, it gives you the opportunity to hide away and get some alone time. If a social event is planned in advance, a lot of autistic people may say yes initially but then end up finding some excuse to cancel at the last minute – what seemed like a good idea two weeks ago may not be on the day, especially if you struggle to know how you will feel in the future. Many autistic people feel anxious about the idea of socializing as there are so many factors to consider – social, sensory, change, energy it takes up etc. There are not many parts of socializing that are simple when you are autistic, and all of the potential impacts need to be taken into consideration so that a decision can be made on whether or not it's worth it.

With all of this being said, there are also many autistic people who have no desire to complicate their lives with people and social events. They will say no to everything, possibly due to a lack of social imagination (not knowing what something will be like so not wanting to risk being out of their comfort zone), having no energy to spend time with people outside of the necessities such as work, education, or family, or because they just love to spend their free time alone engaging in their interests uninterrupted. We live in a world that is constantly telling us that we need to have a big social life and circle, however, if you don't there is nothing wrong with that and it doesn't make you a sociopath.

The amount of time autistic people can cope in social situations does appear to be quite different to non-autistic people, and many feel they have a much more limited capacity for socializing (some call it a social battery), even with people they really love spending time with. For some, socializing is likely to need to be done in a managed way or the impact on them can result in needing hours or days of people-free time. The amount of downtime needed in order to recoup will depend on many factors including the length of time they have been socializing, what the activity was, who it was with, and what else they have been doing recently. This lack of capacity can be very noticeable for people who have a busy home life. You may love your partner and children very much, but even they can drain your resources (and that's OK to admit). If you have a job as well, you are likely to be peopled out all the time as you do not have as many opportunities to get the peace and quiet that you need. Even if you do not have such a busy home life, going to work where there are many people that you have to interact with on a daily basis can also impact your ability to socialize in your spare time. If you are spending your working days with colleagues/customers, it can lead to a complete depletion of your social battery making it difficult to maintain other relationships. Some autistic people describe their social battery running out like a switch going off quite suddenly and they can no longer participate in the social event, leading them to need to leave very quickly and sometimes without even saying goodbye. The social switch goes off and you're out of there!

One way some deal with wanting personal relationships but in a very managed way is to have online friends. Online friendships can be switched off when the social battery is low. There is less of an expectation to be constantly present and it is also easier to dip in and out of conversations.

Even though this is by no means universal in the autistic population, there are those who would much rather spend their time with animals over humans, and for good reason. People have incredible bonds with their animals and feel very safe around them due to a lack of judgement or having to navigate complex social rules. Animals do not really care about anything other than having their basic needs met (food, affection, shelter, exercise). Sounds perfect, eh?!

Again, not universal, but for some having friendships with those who are considerably older or younger seems to prove easier. Common remarks are that people outside of their age group are less judgemental, more interesting, and have similar hobbies. If you are someone who is not hitting the stereotypical life milestones (marriage, children, job, own house etc.), you may feel more accepted if you spend your time with people who are living life in a similar way. When people have similar life experiences they tend to have more commonality, and this could be why autistic people are drawn to other neurodivergent people. If a lot of this book resonates with you, you may also start realizing that many of the people around you could also be neurodivergent.

Every autistic person's motivations for how they socialize, or not, are different and, like with everything, may change over time. Your motivations may include (but are not limited to) only wanting to do certain activities, only spending time with a select few people, not wanting to mix people from different areas of your life, needing to take on a role, only meeting with people one-to-one, needing to see people for a set amount of time, or not wanting to see people at all.

Masking Autistic Traits

The idea of masking or camouflaging autistic traits was briefly discussed earlier in this chapter, and it is something that researchers (Hull et al., 2018; Lai et al., 2016; Livingston et al., 2019; Miller et al., 2021) have all studied since it is now widely recognized as something that autistic people do to compensate for their differences in a neuronormative world. Hull et al. (2018) developed the Camouflaging Autistic Traits Questionnaire self-report test (CAT-Q) to assess both autistic and non-autistic people's levels of masking (there is more information on the CAT-Q in Chapter 7 and a link to an online test in the Resources section at the end of the book).

In short, masking is implementing both conscious and subconscious actions to change aspects of yourself by hiding your autistic traits in order to fit in socially (Hull et al., 2018, p. 819). The list of how autistic people mask is incredibly long and varies between individuals, and there is some evidence that people who identify as female mask more than those who identify as male (Livingston et al., 2019, p. 766). Some of the strategies that people may use include mimicking body language and mannerisms, accents and tone of voice, eye contact, interests, 'energy' (being more introverted or extroverted depending on who they are with), and even dress sense and interests. Other compensatory methods may include implementing strategies gathered from not just real-life interactions but also from TV programmes and films, and people may use phrases they have memorized from these in their everyday conversations or emulate fictional characters. For many autistic people, they have spent a lifetime observing people and trying to replicate the behaviours of those they feel understand how to socialize and do so effectively. This then leads them to being able to blend into many different social groups with apparent ease – another term for this is being a social chameleon. On the surface these autistic people appear to be able to socialize effectively but they often feel like the external presentation does not match how they feel internally, and because of this the people they interact with do not understand the toll or effort it takes to continually mask who they really are (Livingston et al., 2019, p. 771). Their ability to mask may also be impacted by other external factors, and if they are feeling particularly tired, anxious, or overwhelmed, or are experiencing sensory overload, they may not be as successful (Livingston et al., 2019, p. 771). Many autistic people start to mask from a young age once they start to realize how different they are to their peers. As mentioned in the communication section of this chapter, everyone masks, whether you are autistic or not, but the amount of masking and the impact this has on autistic people appears to be bigger. It is also not uncommon for autistic people to drink alcohol or take drugs in order to socialize, using it as a 'social crutch'. This, again, is a type of masking.

Romantic Relationships

It will come as no surprise to you but you can be autistic and be in or desire a romantic relationship – you may even have had many relationships – it certainly doesn't make you any less autistic. After all, autism is genetic so autistic people must be procreating, otherwise autism would have died out a long time ago! The rules around dating and progressing romantic relationships may be easier to navigate as they are slightly more obvious than platonic relationships, and therefore you may find it easier to have a partner than friends. But like all relationships, romantic ones can still be tricky and draining as they involve another person demanding things from you, and people are pretty unpredictable. The first stages of a relationship may bring confusion, if you have no idea when people are attracted to you or if they are flirting with you, especially if you meet outside of a dating app or website. If you meet someone on a dating site, you have a better idea of why they are there and what they might want, making it slightly less ambiguous. It may also be that the autistic person thinks they are flirting with someone but their actions aren't being perceived in the way they are hoping. Have you ever been told you are poor at flirting? Maybe this is why!

Empathy

Autistic people can be very compassionate and really want to support those close to them; however, they may not always know exactly what the other person is feeling or how to respond. This can lead to feelings of confusion and that you're not good enough if it feels like you are constantly getting things wrong even though you try hard. Many autistic people love finding solutions to problems so they can fix them, and this can also be the case when it comes to people – it may feel more beneficial to offer something tangible, like a distraction, or a solution, such as finding them a new job, rather than just to listen and say 'oh that sounds awful'. The support you offer people may be based on what you value when you are facing a problem, which is more likely to receive support in a practical way, rather than just having someone say everything will be OK – being placated may feel empty and not overly useful. You may also relate their situation to something similar that has happened in the past to you. This is normally to show that you can understand what they are going through, even though this is not always appreciated by the other person (it can make the other person feel like you are making their problem about you even though that is rarely the case).

Trying to find one definitive definition for empathy is almost impossible (Fletcher-Watson and Bird, 2019, p. 3). The general idea of empathy is that people have an innate ability to know what someone is feeling and understand why they feel/react in a certain way. The stereotypical trope is that autistic people have little to no empathy, but there is a school of thought that goes against this theory. The idea of the double empathy problem is that autistic people can relate, empathize, and communicate much more effectively with other autistic people, as they are more likely to do so in a similar way and have had similar life experiences (Milton, 2012). Milton's theory therefore dispels the idea that autistic people lack empathy, but instead posits that the problem arises when people of different neurotypes try to empathize with each other. In a nutshell; neurotypical + autistic = lack of empathy with each other; autistic + autistic = empathy. If you also have alexithymia (an inability to understand and name your own emotions), it can be incredibly difficult to know how someone else is feeling and what they are experiencing since you can't even identify your own emotions (more on alexithymia later in the book).

Lying

Lying comes in many different forms, from small jokes that seem insignificant to full on deception, and whatever the lie is it can have a big impact on an autistic person if they do not pick up on this straightaway. The small lies, jokes, or sarcasm that are missed may leave you feeling a bit silly or naive, but if you do not understand when someone has a serious ulterior motive it can lead to people taking advantage of you in life-changing ways – being financially scammed, assaulted, or being subjected to control or abuse in relationships (family, work, education, friends, romantically). This leads a lot of autistic people to feel vulnerable because of their trust in other people to have their best intentions in mind, and they may only realize that they have been deceived after the fact or when another person points this out to them. Even though some lies seem silly and harmless to the person telling them, it can end up leaving an autistic person feeling negatively about themselves if they have, once again, fallen for something that is very obvious to other people. Many autistic people do not see the point in lying and therefore do not do it themselves – as was mentioned in the communication section, they feel honesty is the best policy – and may not be able to comprehend why someone would feel the need to lie. If you have been lied to many times and not realized it until it is too late, this can lead to not trusting anyone and questioning everything that is said in order to protect yourself from being deceived. This does not mean that you can necessarily tell when someone is being dishonest, but feel it is safer to not believe anything anyone says unless you have a vast amount of evidence to back it up.

Eye Contact and Facial Affect

Eye contact is one of those weird social rules that adults try to drill into children from a very young age, as not making and maintaining eye contact is considered rude, disrespectful, or a sign you're not listening (by neuronormative standards, and not in all cultures). However, for many autistic people, eye contact is uncomfortable, distracting, and for some even physically painful. It may also be considered pointless if the autistic person does not get any useful information from reading facial expressions. A lot of autistic people can force themselves to maintain eye contact but behind the scenes their inner-chatter may be going crazy trying to monitor their eye contact. When someone is consciously monitoring themselves, they are unlikely to actually be able to concentrate fully and process what is being said to them. Many autistic people choose a particular area of the face that is not the eyes to focus on, such as an ear, the nose, or forehead, therefore feigning eye contact which can make conversing feel less intense. It is also likely to be much more comfortable to sporadically look away, especially when talking; it may be easier to access your thoughts when speaking if you look away as you are not having to try to process additional visual information. Autistic people who are particularly sensitive to eye contact can also find it hard to look at the eyes of people on the television or even look at themselves in the mirror. Even though most autistic people do not enjoy making and maintaining eye contact, there are those who have been told that it is rude not to make eye contact so often – and as they are not sure what the appropriate amount is – they end up staring intensely.

It seems that the difference between autistic and neurotypical eye contact is that for neurotypical people it appears to be a subconscious act that comes naturally to them without much thought, and they also get some form of reward from shared eye contact. In contrast, when autistic people make eye contact it is often a learned or forced behaviour, which in fact can be very distracting and tiring. It's just another process to have to think about and constantly adjust. Not making eye contact can also put you at a disadvantage in social situations, especially romantic ones, such as not noticing someone is flirting with you if you are avoiding their gaze.

As previously mentioned in the communication section, a lot of autistic people can have quite a neutral facial affect, with their external presentation not matching how they are feeling – e.g., looking like they're not enjoying themselves when they are. In contrast, there are those who may not be able to hide or fake how they are feeling, as this shows immediately via their facial affect, which they have little control over. Neurotypical people are generally able to manage their facial expressions, which in turn can protect the feelings of others, whereas autistic people may find this more difficult and have to put in a lot of effort to do so. Some autistic people also talk about being shocked at how they look in photographs, as they look upset or angry even if they are having a lovely time. Some autistic people may practise facial expressions and train themselves to react in a more socially acceptable way, and may observe how others do this so they can replicate it in the future.

Flexibility of Thought/Executive Functioning

Flexibility of thought and executive functioning refers to a group of skills that help you to carry out daily tasks and activities. These skills include planning, time management, organization, multi-tasking, decision making, and remembering details. It is said that autistic people have differences in these areas, often referred to as people having 'executive dysfunction' or inflexible thought patterns. Autistic people generally feel more comfortable when they have some sense of knowing what will happen next and how something will be, which can be achieved by repeating familiar activities and asking for, or researching, information regarding where they are going, how they will get there and how it will be. The systems autistic people put in place are like scaffolding – they help keep everything in place and keep their world safe.

The neuronormative world can cause a lot of problems for autistic people, especially when they cannot implement the systems they have devised and they are forced to be flexible in a way that does not suit them. This can lead to feeling overwhelmed and out of control, which can impact how someone communicates and their ability to navigate the world.

As you go through this section you may notice how many overlaps there are between each section – each one affects everything else, maybe more so than any other part of the diagnostic criteria. We have tried to split it up as neatly as possible.

Flexibility of Thought and Executive Functioning Differences in Childhood

The need for predictability and information can be seen from childhood. As children, of any neurotype, do not have control over their environments or lives, this poses an issue for autistic children who really crave certainty. One way to get certainty is to gather information, and for some children they may ask a lot of questions about absolutely everything. Where are we going? What are we doing? Who is going to be there? etc., etc. As is the case in adulthood, which is discussed later on in this section, autistic children need to prepare themselves for every eventuality, hence the question asking. Information is key! When children reach school age, they may start to implement their own routines and plans, such as getting their school bag ready the night before, laying out their clothes, organizing toys/ books, or coming up with colour coded revision timetables. Even though this can give them some semblance of control, change will still impact them in a negative way. If plans then change with little to no information given in advance, this can cause autistic children to become very overwhelmed and have what some people refer to as a meltdown. Meltdowns are another term for a tantrum, but in the context of autism, they refer to behaviour displayed by someone when they become overwhelmed. Meltdowns are normally triggered by one event but it is likely not just that one particular incident that has caused the meltdown – it will be the build-up of many different things, including sensory overwhelm, change to routines, or too many social interactions.

In general, autistic children enjoy lining up, organizing, and categorizing their possessions. They will have set ways in which they line up their toys and they will notice – and not be amused – if someone moves one. They may enjoy experimenting with different systems in order to categorize certain items such as books, marbles, or building blocks. Many autistic children also enjoy having collections of items, and feel very satisfied if they manage to collect the full set. A lot of autistic children love playing with Lego sets, but prefer to follow the instructions and may not be able or want to make up their own buildings, vehicles, or scenes. Once the set is made, they are more likely to want to display it rather than taking it to pieces and reusing them for another project. Autistic children may also have a tendency for more repetitive play, and enjoy doing the same activity or watching/reading the same thing over and over again.

Just like in adulthood, decision making in childhood can pose issues, and you may have memories of becoming really overwhelmed in a sweet or toy shop when you had a bit of pocket money. The vast majority of decisions that a child needs to make do not tend to have significant implications, but children can still feel very overwhelmed if there are too many options available and they are worried about regretting their choice of what toy or sweets to buy. Autistic children are more likely to choose something they are familiar with as they know exactly what they are getting and then there are no shocks. This can show in actions such as watching the same film/TV show on repeat, always choosing the same cup, or only wanting to wear blue socks (the action itself is not important, it's the need for it that is).

Autistic children can have very fixed ideas on what is right and wrong – otherwise known as black-and-white or all-or-nothing thinking. This may be displayed in rule following and getting irate if people – of any age – break the rules, which may cause them to tell off adults or their peers, without considering the idea of hierarchy, authority, or social consequences. For many autistic children, the rules have to make sense or benefit them, otherwise they will not follow them. Let's take cheating in a board game as an example – the need to win might override the need to follow the rules, so you may decide that in this instance cheating is fine. However, if someone else cheated... game over, with shouts of 'that's not fair!', and possibly a flipped board. Having a strong sense of justice and fairness is another autistic trait that can be very apparent from childhood. Another way black-and-white thinking can be exhibited in autistic children, like in adulthood, is a need to be right, all the time. Autistic children will argue their point and it will not matter how much information or evidence is given to the contrary; they are likely never to concede.

Routines and Planning in Adulthood

As mentioned in the introduction to this part of the diagnostic criteria, the motivation to plan and have routines tends to be a need for certainty and knowing what is going to happen in as many aspects of your life as possible. If you have these things it is then easier (but not always pleasant) to deal with the bits that do change. Everybody's routines are likely to differ, with some routines being very fixed such as getting up at set times, getting the same bus to work, walking the dog the same route. Whereas others will be looser, having set days to do certain tasks but not times. Routines are not limited to doing the same thing at the same time of day but can also include the specific way in which you carry out tasks. An example of this type of routine would be how you get dressed in the morning and, for some, they will have a specific order that they put their clothes on and they will not deviate from it. It is also common for autistic people to have the same breakfast, lunch, and/or dinner on a daily basis or have a weekly meal plan that tends to consist of a small number of different meals that have been deemed safe. There may also be a routine with how you eat each item on your plate (best till last is common), along with the crockery, mugs, and cutlery used. Whatever the routine is, it provides certainty and predictability, and takes away the need for decision making (more on that later). Knowing exactly what is going to be happening means that you can prepare yourself for the day, week, and months ahead.

Autistic people, on the whole, love to and need to plan pretty much everything, as it provides them with a framework to go about daily activities and tasks. When you have a plan, you have more information and control over your life and do not have to make on-the-spot decisions about what to wear, what to eat, or where to go. When there is free time, such as weekends or days off work, a new plan/structure may need to be put in place or usual routines adhered to as closely as possible. It can be hard to know what to do in your free time if there is nothing planned as there are too many potential options which can feel overwhelming. It doesn't matter which method or system you use to plan, the fact you need to is enough. Plans are even more important when you are leaving the comfort of your home and going on holiday, where you cannot carry out your normal routines. When going on holiday, the planning stage may consist of in-depth research months in advance, with information being recorded so that daily itineraries and packing lists can be made. The idea of going away on holiday to new places can be too overwhelming for some autistic people, so they will prefer to go to the same place every time as they know exactly what to expect and do not need to spend time and energy on planning.

Due to this need to plan and know exactly what is going to happen, many autistic people have a strong aversion to spontaneity and surprises, which can be anything from receiving gifts, to being thrown a surprise party, to someone suggesting going out at the last minute, or even roadworks on the way to work. When things are spontaneous they do not give the time to mentally or physically prepare in advance which can cause distress. Some autistic people (including one of your authors) read the plots and spoilers for movies online before going to the cinema so that they know what is going to happen and don't have to worry about becoming upset or surprised.

Change

On the whole, autistic people do not like imposed changes (changes that are caused by external factors) but can cope more with self-imposed change (changes that they have decided to implement). Even if the change imposed will result in a better outcome, it is still likely to be met with resistance at first.

Some big life events, such as going away on holiday, moving house, or getting a new job, are particularly disruptive as there is not just a change to routines but also to the environment people are in. These situations may take an autistic person longer to adapt to compared to someone who is neurotypical, as they will need to try to implement new routines and systems to provide them with the certainty that they crave. But it's not just big changes such as these that cause issues. Even things that most of the population would just deal with can cause stress and anxiety, such as the supermarket running out of the specific washing powder that you normally use or someone else being late. The reason change causes anxiety and resistance is because autistic people tend not to be able to shift from one thing to another quickly. It can be harder to switch between tasks if you do not like change, as you do not have the time to re-adjust and plan for what needs to be done next. This is especially the case at work or home if someone asks you to stop what you are doing and start something new straightaway. As previously discussed, when making a decision or a plan, it takes time for an autistic person to process all of the possible outcomes and potential impacts it will have on them. So when something changes – big or small – all of this hard work is undone and they have to start from scratch. This process is very tiring and time consuming.

Decision Making

As adults we have to make a multitude of decisions on a daily basis, about all sorts of different things, which is something that autistic people can find very difficult, regardless of the importance of the decision. It is not like in childhood when the most important decision you have to make is what sweets to have or toys to buy. Every day we have to decide what to wear, eat, watch on the TV, what tasks are priorities. This daily process can be exhausting if it's something you struggle with, and even more so if you have to make decisions on behalf of children or other family members. It appears that one underlying reason for finding decision making stressful is a fear of getting it 'wrong', which can lead people to have 'decision paralysis' – when you become overwhelmed by all of the possibilities, resulting in you not being able to make any decision at all and feeling stuck. This is why keeping life simple is a good idea, such as if you have the same foods at mealtimes each day, or a meal plan; then you do not have to think about what to cook each day, so there are three less decisions to make. Choosing familiar and known options not only removes the decision making process, but also the uncertainty and potential for change. Once you have found something that you know you enjoy, whether that's a type of shampoo, brand of pasta, the perfect running route, or pair of pants, why on earth would you risk changing it to something potentially inferior, stressful, or boring?

Decision making without all of the information is almost impossible. When purchasing a new item, autistic people generally need to go on an information gathering mission so that they can make the most informed decision possible. This need for information means that autistic people are generally not impulsive, and even if you look like you are to the people around you, it is likely that you are constantly doing a lot of processing of information, internet searches and the like in order to reach the point you have. Anecdotally, it appears that autistic people would prefer to have fewer options available to them to choose from as there is then less to weigh up.

This is where repeated choices, plans, and rules become very useful. If you know what you are going to be doing, eating, wearing, you do not have to make as many decisions each day. Planning in advance also helps with transitioning from one task to another as you know exactly what comes next and have curated your day in a way that suits you. Some autistic people also come up with their own rules for criteria when needing to make a decision, which could include deferring to other people. If they defer the process to someone else, it is then out of their control, but this is easier than having to weigh up everything and potentially make the wrong choice. When needing to make snap decisions such as ordering food, always making the same choice will alleviate some of the anxiety.

Pattern Spotting, Attention to Detail, and Systems
A lot of autistic people have amazing attention to detail and have used this strength to have very successful careers where this is valued – computer programmers, analysts, graphic designers, therapists, architects, engineers etc. This ability to spot patterns and be attuned to the finer details is likely to apply not only in the workplace, but also in their personal life as well. Some autistic people may spot

patterns with how people behave, car registration plates, or notice when there is something very slightly different in their environment. Where it can sometimes cause problems is when their attention is focused purely on the finer details because they are more interesting or feel more important, leaving the bigger picture overlooked. A somewhat silly example of missing the bigger picture in everyday life is hanging out the washing. For many autistic people they will have a very set way that this task (or any other) is carried out, and it can be frustrating when someone else does it in a different way. The detail (the *way* the washing is hung up) is more important than the bigger picture (the clothes are hung up and drying). In practice, for the end result of dry clothes to be achieved, it does not actually matter that all the socks are hung out with the same coloured pegs, but for many autistic people this is not the case – the system itself is just as important as the end result. Everyone's reasons for doing tasks in a specific way may be different, however, a lot of autistic systems are based around efficiency. Loading the dishwasher is done in a way that makes the most of the space; the shopping list is written in order of where items appear in the supermarket so as not to miss anything or have to visit an aisle twice; clothes are put away so it is easier to see what to wear. When things are efficient, it saves not only time but brain power as well.

Rigidity of Thought

Autistic people who have a black-and-white/all-or-nothing thinking style tend to have very fixed views and opinions on a range of topics that are important to them. This is likely to start in childhood, as previously mentioned, but the subject matter will change over time. They may still need to have control over their environment, have set systems to carry out tasks like doing the washing up/loading the dishwasher, and still need to follow rules, but may also start to form strong opinions around different topics such as politics and religion. It doesn't matter what the opinion is, once one has been formed, the likelihood of it changing or them being able to see an alternative perspective or ways of doing things is slim. For a lot of autistic people they may not understand why someone thinks or does something in a different way to them because they feel their way is the most logical, and therefore the best and only way. These thought patterns are not because autistic people are stubborn, even though it can be perceived that way, but because they like to gather as much information as possible so that they can make the best decision possible. At times, it can feel like other people just haven't done the same level of research or have not found the missing piece that they have.

On occasion, having rigid all-or-nothing thinking can cause autistic people to no longer communicate with people if someone's actions go against their principles, ethics, values, or they feel the other person has been unfair and unjust, even if they have been friends for many years. It can be hard for the autistic person to see beyond the sense of being wronged and remember the redeeming features of the person and the relationship. This doesn't just apply to other people's actions, but may also apply to your own – you may feel that you are a failure if you get lower marks than you were expecting on a test, even if you have passed, or if you make one small mistake at work. In these examples, there is no grey area, and it is perceived that you are good or bad, right or wrong, succeeding or failing.

In general, autistic people do not like being wrong, and admitting that they are is even worse. Every human makes mistakes, and some people find this easier to accept than others. Autistic people may need a lot of evidence of their error, from multiple trusted sources, as they are unlikely to just accept what one person has said to them if they are adamant that they were right.

Sensory

In order to meet the diagnostic criteria for autism you do not need to have differences with all of the senses, just one or more, and to a degree which impacts your daily life. This is part of the criteria for both the DSM-5 and the ICD-11. Everyone's sensory profile will be unique, and may include both avoidant behaviours (hypersensitivity) and seeking behaviours (hyposensitivity). There are the main senses of sight, hearing, smell, taste, and touch, as well as pain, temperature, interoception (internal signals related to hunger, thirst, and going to the bathroom), and synaesthesia which is a crossover of the senses, such as seeing the colour blue when you hear the word 'bed'.

Most non-autistic people do not have a need to control their sensory environment to the level that autistic people do. We are not implying that all non-autistic people have no sensory sensitivities, just that the impact on them may not be as great (unless someone has a sensory processing disorder which is discussed in Chapter 6, What Else Could It Be?).

It is not so much about *what* the preference is but the fact that *there is* a preference that is important. When making your notes, consider what the sense is, the effect that the sense has on you, strategies you may use – you may not realize that you have strategies, such as avoiding travelling or shopping at certain times of the day, along with the impact this has on a daily basis. There is more about how to go about this in Chapter 11, It's a Yes, Now What? It is also common for autistic people to not even realize that what they are experiencing is considerably different to those around them.

Sight

Many autistic individuals express hypersensitivity to light and tend to have a preference for lower level lighting at home and at work, or wear tinted glasses to compensate. People often comment on not enjoying having the 'big light' on (main ceiling light), and struggling in brightly lit places, especially with fluorescent tube lighting. They tend to favour using lamps and prefer warmer lighting rather than white light. There are also others who experience hyposensitivity to light and who seek out very bright or flashing lights, which they may find soothes and calms them; however, this does appear to be less common.

People affected by bright lights combat their hypersensitivity by wearing sunglasses/hats, and controlling the levels of lighting they are subject to, such as using lamps at home, requesting that the light above their desk is switched off at work, or choosing where they sit in a restaurant or cinema. Sensory differences with light can also affect sleep, and some people need a completely dark room in order to go to sleep, with this being obtained by using a blackout eye mask or curtains.

Hearing

Some autistic people report being able to pick up on very subtle noises that others may not notice. These could include being acutely aware of the ticking of a clock, dripping tap, or even the electrical hum of plug sockets, power lines, and appliances. They may also have an issue with loud sudden noises, with many people feeling the need to put their fingers in their ears when an emergency vehicle goes past with the siren on, or a kettle whistles. These people usually did not enjoy fireworks shows or playing with balloons as children.

Multiple sources of sounds can also be overwhelming, whether that's at home or when out in public. This overload of noises makes it difficult to focus on the task at hand or the conversation you are trying to have with the person you are with. In an office or educational setting, this can lead to becoming increasingly distracted and unable to concentrate on work.

One of the most common complaints about sound is the lack of control over environmental noise. People may counteract this by listening to loud music via headphones to block out sounds and have control over the auditory environment. Some autistic people also find that listening to music that they enjoy can be relaxing.

Other strategies autistic people may use to combat their sound sensitivity include using one of the many different types of ear plugs on the market – some of which are made especially with neurodivergent people in mind – noise-cancelling headphones, or white noise machines.

Smell

Autistic people's reaction to different smells varies, and there is no definitive list of what every autistic person likes and dislikes. In general, autistic people will have a strong reaction when they smell something they like or dislike. That being said, many autistic people do dislike synthetic or strong scents such as air fresheners, reed diffusers, perfumes/aftershaves, or laundry products, and may avoid visiting certain shops or being in environments where other people are cooking. Their reaction to smells they do not like may include headaches, feeling sick, or being able to taste them. Autistic people may also seek out their favourite smells, which could include scented candles, essential oils, or something more unusual such as petrol or unwashed socks. This can have a soothing or calming effect on them, in the same way listening to music does. Some autistic people have a 'strong nose' or sensitive sense of smell, and can pick up on subtle smells that other people do not notice. These include being able to smell when food is about to go off, a gas leak, or what someone has had for dinner just by the smell on their clothes.

Taste

One of the stereotypical views about autistic people is that they are very selective about the food and drink they consume and may be described as 'picky eaters'. For some autistic people this is certainly true and they may have a preference for 'beige' food – foods with bland flavours that are always consistent in appearance, taste, and texture. The texture of food is often equally as important, if not more, for autistic people; some may enjoy the taste of certain foods but have a very strong aversion to the texture. If there are any unexpected tastes or textures this may cause someone to be unable to eat the rest of their meal for fear of it happening again.

Autistic people do not just avoid foods and drinks; they may also seek out certain flavours and textures. In order for the consistency of texture and flavour to be guaranteed, it is safer to only eat specific brands of a food or cook meals in the same way every time. There are certain foods that are always consistent, such as pizza, chicken nuggets, plain rice, or pasta. However, foods such as vegetables and fruit may be too unpredictable as there are so many potential variations even when they come out of the same box. Whilst one strawberry may be perfect, the next one out of the same punnet could be too sweet/sour/soft/hard. This is only something you can find out once you have taken a bite and this is likely to be too much of a risk. Alongside the preferences that autistic people have on what they are eating is how the food is served. Some people need the different items of food on their plate to not be touching so there is no contamination, and some like it when it's all mixed up so that all food items are mixed together and each mouthful is identical in taste and texture. The order in which people eat their meals may also be important to them, and this was briefly mentioned in the chapter on the diagnostic criteria. Everyone has different strategies, which could include: leaving the best bite till last so you always finish on your favourite taste; eating all of one item at a time before moving on to the next so there is no flavour/texture mixes; having a bit of everything on the fork at once; and others – once a person told us that they ate their food alphabetically.

If you do not live in your native country, but grew up somewhere with different food types and flavours from where you now reside, it is important to think about whether your food preferences would be seen as unusual in your home country.

Touch

Many autistic people have specific needs regarding touch and what they seek out and avoid, which does not just come in the form of physical contact with people, but also with materials/clothing, and items in the environment. From childhood, some autistic people may have a strong aversion to wearing certain items of clothing, and may have become distressed when putting on school uniforms, jeans, or tights. This sensory difference to clothing can last into adulthood, and some autistic people need to cut the labels out of their clothes, wear socks inside out or prefer ones without any seams, have a preference for looser fitting clothes like hoodies and joggers, or do not like tight, restrictive items. When you are hypersensitive to touch you will notice everything that you find uncomfortable or scratchy, which can be both distracting and distressing. Obviously, every autistic person's preference will vary but common materials mentioned that people strongly dislike are wool, velvet, velour, cotton wool, polyester, and microfiber, and the materials that are sought out tend to be softer or made of natural fibres such as cotton. Because of this, many autistic people dislike work and school uniforms as they tend to be made out of synthetic materials that are more likely to be itchy or make you sweat.

It is not just the feel of certain textiles that autistic people may have an aversion to, but also other substances like creams, water, and foods. It may be that they dislike doing the washing up due to having to touch old, soggy food, or they don't like having a shower/bath or going swimming due to not liking the feeling of being wet afterwards. They may feel they have to be completely dry before being able to get dressed as they do not like the feeling of dry clothing touching wet skin. Some autistic children hate having suncream applied due to the stickiness of it, and as adults may choose not to use body lotions or face creams for this reason. When cooking, some autistic people need to use rubber gloves because they have an aversion to the feel of raw meat/fish or other food items. Along with the feel of foods, they may also have an aversion to having things on their hands in general, not due to germs but because they do not like the feeling of having something sticky, gritty, or oily on them. This can also be the case when in the garden or visiting the beach – many autistic people do not enjoy having sand on their body or mud on their hands.

Some autistic people feel a need to 'even up' touch, either from other people or if they bump into something. Meaning when one part or side of the body makes contact with someone or something, the same sensation needs to be replicated on the other side of the body, making the sensation symmetrical. Another phenomenon is if a light touch is received, firm touch needs to then be applied to counteract the less desirable light touch. We have also heard of autistic people feeling like the imprint of a hand is still on them after being touched by someone, which can cause discomfort. The amount of pressure of the touch is important, with every autistic person having their own preference. Utilizing weighted blankets or receiving a firm hug/squeeze appears to calm the nervous system for some, but not all.

Not all autistic people avoid physical contact, but as with many of the senses, control can be important. Some may only avoid physical contact with people that they do not know or when they are feeling overwhelmed, but seek it out from people they are close to and comfortable with.

Pain

Autistic people can have either higher or lower than typical tolerance levels to pain. When someone has a very high pain threshold, they may not realize that they have broken a bone or seriously injured themselves. They may also have no issues with long tattooing sessions (yes, autistic people can like tattoos!). If someone has a low pain tolerance, they may have been accused of being overly sensitive, especially as a child, as they would cry at the slightest bump. They may also need much more pain relief medication when having operations, procedures, or if they have a headache.

Temperature

For some autistic people they find it difficult to regulate their body temperature, often feeling too hot or cold, when others around them may feel the opposite. They may not like summer time or being in hot environments, due to feeling the heat acutely which can make the skin feel 'prickly' and make them sweat. The feel of the sweat can also cause sensory overload, as well as the damp clothes this can cause. People who dislike being cold may have very hot showers, and need many layers of clothing or blankets even in summer.

Other Sensory Differences Not Listed in the DSM-5 or ICD-11
Interoception (Internal Signals)

Interoception is the ability to recognize the internal signals from your body when you are feeling hungry, thirsty, tired, or if you need the toilet, which is something that many autistic people can have difficulties with. For many, they will only notice these signals when they have become exaggerated – feeling dizzy or sick due to not eating, developing a headache from dehydration, becoming desperate for the toilet, or nodding off unexpectedly – or if someone reminds them to meet their body's needs. It can be annoying to have to meet your body's needs when you are engaged in your interests, so some people will just ignore these needs until they have no choice but to attend to them.

Synaesthesia

Synaesthesia is a fairly rare phenomenon, affecting less than 5% of the population, both autistic and non-autistic (Simner et al., 2006, p. 1028). It is where two or more senses are activated at the same time. For example, someone hears a word and then sees a colour. There are over 60 different types of synaesthesia (Brang and Ramachandran, 2011, p. 2). The following are the most frequent that we have come across, but that's not to say that these are the most common in general:

- Day/colour or month/colour – Associating different days of the week with different colours
- Grapheme/colour – Associating different letters (graphemes) with different colours
- Auditory/tactile – Hearing a sound and feeling a sensation in the body
- Hearing/motion – Hearing sounds when movement is seen
- Sound/colour – Hearing a sound, such as music, when seeing colours
- Mirror/touch – Physically feeling something that you have witnessed happen to someone else (i.e., they stub their toe, you feel pain in the same toe)

Synaesthetes (people with synaesthesia) are likely to have more than one type. It is lifelong, involuntary, and tends not to change over time. For the most part, it is an enjoyable experience, unless many senses are being triggered at once which can cause sensory overload (Bogdashina, 2016).

Intense Interests

The difference between neurotypical hobbies and autistic intense interests is the depth, thought, and time put into them and the joy they generate. If you have a look on social media, there are a lot of autistic people talking about 'autistic joy', which is the intense feeling someone who is autistic gets when engaging in their interest. Autistic interests can be focused on absolutely anything and are not solely based around trains, planes, and dinosaurs as the stereotypical trope may suggest. A person's specific interest could start in childhood and be lifelong, whilst others may switch between many interests over time.

As mentioned above, the intensity of the interest is the key, not the topic. As an example, let's take football. Lots of people all over the world are very keen supporters of a football team, local or national. A neurotypical person may go to the pub to watch their team, or even have a season ticket, check the scores, and keep up with the team. An autistic person will do all of this as well as researching all of the match and player statistics, have an encyclopaedic knowledge of how their team has performed in every season for the last 30 years, collect match day memorabilia and merchandise, and want to talk at length about it to everyone who takes even the slightest bit of interest in their team. Now replace 'football' with your topic of interest... sound familiar?

There are autistic people whose intense interest is to do with people, which can include psychology, true crime, famous people, and TV shows – all of which can provide a learning database of information about people and how they think and behave, which is highly useful in everyday life. Autistic people spend a lifetime trying to learn and understand the neuronormative social rules, which can lead to human behaviour becoming an intense interest. This has even led to some having very successful careers as therapists, psychologists, and mental health practitioners.

Many autistic people also report experiencing limerence, defined as an obsessive level of romantic interest in a person, which could be someone they know, have only met once, or have never met such as a celebrity. The person that they desire will dominate their thoughts, and they will feel a need to gain in-depth information on their life, using their phenomenal research skills to do so. Limerence can start at any age; the thoughts of those affected will be consumed by this person, and they will create an imaginary world with them in it, potentially for escapism.

A lot of people believe they do not have any intense interests as they do not fit the stereotype of having a fixed lifelong enthusiasm based on a single subject. Instead, they are more likely to have intense transient interests – short-term passions which can last for any length of time but will end at some point. The steep learning curve of a new topic appears to be the most enjoyable aspect of these short-er-lived interests. You get to deep dive into a topic, researching, buying everything you need, spending every free waking hour consumed by it, until you reach a point where you can no longer learn any more without having to attend a class; you get to an almost expert level of knowledge and there is not much left to learn, or you get bored and move on to something new and exciting. If you tend to have intense transient interests, you are likely to have a bookshelf full of half or never read books on a vast array of subjects, and a cupboard full of equipment and a lot of half-finished projects.

Repetitive Movements/Stimming

Repetitive movements or stimming are self-soothing behaviours that take many forms, and may change throughout life. These can include motor stims such as finger tapping, biting fingernails, picking skin, trichotillomania (pulling out hair), spinning, blinking, twitching, spinning, flapping, and tiptoe walking. Some people may engage in vocal stims which can include throat clearing, coughing, tongue clicking, and echolalia (repetitively making the same sound or saying the same words or phrases). These behaviours may be subtle or exaggerated and made when excited, happy, bored, anxious, or overwhelmed, and regardless of the action or when engaged in it, it will bring them comfort when they need it most. Most stimming actions are voluntary, however, some may be subconscious and therefore difficult to control. It is not uncommon for autistic people to suppress their stims when with other people. This is another form of masking which was discussed earlier in this chapter.

Features Presented Across the Lifespan

One of the key aspects of the diagnostic criteria for autism, in both the ICD-11 and the DSM-5, is that autistic features have to be present from childhood, but may not cause any issues until the pressures of life become too much. The presentation throughout life can change due to a myriad of different factors, including life transitions such as starting a new school, moving house, becoming a parent, getting a new job or not being as well supported in work/education, going through menopause, or other health concerns. These can all affect the coping mechanisms that have been put in place to counteract and deal with any difficulties faced. People do not become more or less autistic, but their ability to manage may change and is directly affected by life and the environment they live in.

It is also quite common for children to only present as autistic in one setting, normally at home due to the level of masking they engage in when at school, which means teachers do not see the impact the school environment has on them. The effect of masking that much can result in what is sometimes called 'the 4pm explosion'. Once the autistic child gets home, where they feel safe to be themselves, they stop being able or needing to mask, and the ramifications of pretending all day at school cause an almighty meltdown. Anecdotally, the reason why some people are not diagnosed as a child is that it can be difficult to pursue a diagnosis if there is no additional evidence from the school or the school is not willing to refer the child for assessment.

If the onset of the majority of the features discussed above came on later in life, or you do not meet the criteria, they are likely to be explained by another condition (please see Chapter 6, What Else Could It Be?).

Final Thoughts on the Diagnostic Criteria

When considering your own autistic traits, be specific about your strengths and differences, what impacts you and what doesn't. You need to meet the criteria as set out in the DSM-5 and ICD-11, but some of the examples that have been discussed throughout this chapter may not apply to you, and it is by no means exhaustive, as there is not enough paper in the world to give examples of every autistic person's experiences.

Every autistic person is different and has different challenges in the world that, as mentioned, are likely to fluctuate throughout their life. The more comprehensive your evidence, the more likely you are to be able to prove to a professional that you are autistic, or even feel confident in self-identifying as autistic.

Self-Assessment for Chapter 2 – Meeting the Diagnostic Criteria

Now that you have read what types of thinking styles and behaviours could be considered to meet the diagnostic criteria for autism, take some notes on the blank pages at the end of the book and decide whether you think you would meet each part of the criteria.

Communication and language ☐ Yes ☐ No

Social relationships ☐ Yes ☐ No

Flexibility of thought/executive functioning ☐ Yes ☐ No

Sensory differences ☐ Yes ☐ No

Intense interests ☐ Yes ☐ No

Repetitive movements ☐ Yes ☐ No

Above features seen across lifespan – childhood and adulthood ☐ Yes ☐ No

Score yourself between 0 and 10 on the likelihood that you are autistic:

. . . .

Chapter 3

What Brings You Here?

COMMON CATALYSTS FOR CONSIDERING AUTISM

There are many reasons why you may have come to start thinking about the possibility you are autistic as an adult. You may well still be in the stage of being in shock with your head spinning and finding it hard to believe. How could you have got to this age in life without someone noticing? It's a common question and experience, so you are not alone. We know that if you were born earlier than 1994, which is when Asperger syndrome was first included in the diagnostic manuals, there was no autism diagnosis that was available for those with no intellectual learning disability, and so you could not have been diagnosed as a child. Asperger syndrome was, simply put, the presence of autistic features without any accompanying low IQ or speech delay. Professor Tony Attwood's *The Complete Guide to Asperger Syndrome* (2008) was the seminal text on the subject and continues to be a valuable and comprehensive resource. We shall later discuss how if you are non-male, non-white, from a lower socioeconomic background or someone who uses compensatory, masked, and learned behaviours, your chances of being noticed as autistic up until recently were even lower. So here you are, wondering if this could possibly explain a whole bunch of stuff about your life.

You may be thinking what's the point in getting a diagnosis at this time in your life, since you have managed to survive this far (and well done for that), and have established yourself in the world for better or for worse. Let us reassure you that it is never too late to have an autism assessment: the oldest person we have assessed was 87 years of age and she said that she wanted to know why she had felt so different before the end of her life. It always has value to know who you are, if not for yourself but for those who may care for you – at any point in your life. For example, it may be important to have an autism diagnosis in your later years so that you are not considered mistakenly to have dementia or depression, or to make sure that your needs and preferences around social interaction or sensory considerations are respected when you may be unable to communicate these.

When we assess people, we always ask 'What brings you here?' to get a sense of what has led to the person taking this big step to seek confirmation through the process of diagnostic assessment, because their answers can sometimes provide evidence and insight into their autistic suspicions. We are interested to know how they came across the idea of autism in relation to themselves, and why they have decided to act upon these thoughts or suspicions at this particular time; there is often a catalyst or event which takes a person from thoughts to action. You know this: that's why you are holding this book. So, in order to give you some context about whether your particular catalytic event is unique or quite common, we have col-lected the most frequently given responses to the question 'What brings you here, and why now?' Your own reasons may not be listed here, but you may be able to relate to some of those given, and this may give you further insight into your own autistic journey. It is often the case that it is not one reason or event that has led to this point, but several, which over time have accumulated to the point that they cannot be disregarded any longer, and some closure or certainty must be sought.

Another quick reminder to take notes, highlight sections, use bookmarks, or whatever your preferred method is in preparation for the self-assessment checklist at the end of the chapter.

I Have Always Felt Different

This is probably the most commonly stated response in our experience of autism assessment. It is usually the first line of the reply to the 'What brings you here?' question. The person may have been aware that they did not fit in socially with their peers at a relatively young age, but had no explanation for this at the time, apart from it being everyone else's fault, or entirely their own. These two explanations can result in either a somewhat superior and arrogant-appearing presentation or an extremely passive profile, often full of self-shame, with an early onset of masking and mimicking in an attempt to become a version of themselves which is palatable to others.

Narratives to explain this persistent apartness may have developed as we try to make sense of our experiences and observe that those around us appear to not be having them. Typically, a person will state that the reasons for their difference were due to being:

- The new kid at school – their family moved a lot
- Living some distance from school so no one could come to play
- An only child
- Significantly more or less academically able
- The only Black/mixed race child in the class
- Taller/shorter/fatter than their peers
- Ginger/wearing glasses/any other obvious physical difference
- From a different culture or first language
- Non-hetero/cis gender conforming
- Having very different and atypical hobbies and interests

The person may have settled on one or more explanations that provide a partial understanding of their experiences, which often include bullying and exclusion – being called 'weird' is very common. They may continue to be satisfied with this narrative well into adulthood, perhaps seeking therapy for the trauma they experienced, as some of the issues from childhood continually replay and repeat into adulthood. For many who describe this trajectory, their long-held narrative begins to crumble, as once free from childhood limitations, they find that they continue to 'feel different' and struggle to fit in with colleagues, peers, neighbours, and to establish friendships and relationships. They may observe others with similar features to those listed above easily integrating into social groups when they cannot. Eventually, they must conclude: there must be another reason: 'Wherever I go and whatever I do, it is the same. The problem must be me'.

This realization can be a point of despair and hopelessness that they are irretrievably broken, that things will never be any different, and that they are alone in being this way. Understandably, this can lead some into depression. Often then what follows is a deep dive into research of all the possible psychological diagnoses and personality profiles that may offer an explanation, and autism may be one of them. This is often initially dismissed as being too crazy to even consider, due to an outdated or narrow perception of what autism can 'look like', but time and time again, it will keep on popping up and can be ignored no longer.

I Am Sure That I Am Autistic, but I Need External Validation

This person has been through all of the earlier steps in their journey to reach the point of self-diagnosis and concluded that they are definitely autistic. If truth be told, this person is usually correct, but feels the need for a second opinion because despite all of their research, screening test scores, and confirmation from those around them, they (and many like them) have a need to go through the assessment process with a diagnostician and receive an 'official' diagnosis. The use of the word 'validation' is common, as is the word 'permission'. The person may say that they are uncomfortable in telling others they are autistic without having gone through a diagnostic assessment and receiving external validation and confirmation; that they feel like a 'fraud' or an 'imposter'. They may be lurking on the fringes of online autism groups and communities but feel unable to join in and contribute because they fear exclusion. For this person, the assessment itself can be fraught with anxiety because despite their certainty, they fear being told that they are not autistic after all, and that they may have to go back to square one in their search for an answer.

A Family Member Has Been Diagnosed as Autistic

In the past, it would sometimes be the case that a parent would attend an autism assessment with their child who had been referred for diagnosis and state 'There is nothing wrong with my child, he is just like me'. It was always the father and always about his son. Thankfully, this doesn't happen quite so often these days, but it still does from time to time (and it's still always the dads who say it so defensively). We now know that autism is highly genetic and inherited and that if you have an autistic child, then there is a good chance that you and/or your partner are autistic yourself – quite often both in our experience. Like seems to attract like in autistic and other neurodivergent relationships, so don't think you can point the finger of blame at each other, Mum and Dad.

What is more often the case these days is that through the process of their child's diagnostic assessment, a parent will reflect on their own childhood and recognize similarities between themselves and their child. Initially, this idea can be resisted as the parent's own understanding of autism may be limited and it is seen as a bad thing, or even a tragedy. They may be asked questions about themselves during their child's assessment and not be comfortable in responding openly about things which are painful or that they feel defensive or shameful about. Over time, their desire to ensure the best support and understanding for their child may lead them to consider their own differences and the impact of these on their relationships, work, and home life. This can be an emotional time and one which may lead to considering autism assessment to gain that clarity and understanding.

My Therapist Suggested I Might Be Autistic

As we know, many autistic people experience mental health challenges throughout their lives, which may include anxiety, depression, obsessive-compulsive disorder, burnout, panic attacks, disordered eating, and others. These difficulties may lead to seeking support from a therapist or other professional. More and more often now, therapists have some knowledge or experience of autism, and quite often when a person is sharing their perceptions and describing how they live their lives, a therapist may see clear features of autism. These may be in the routines that someone lives by, their social networks, their interests, or their sensory requirements. Therapists are usually cautious in suggesting that a person may be autistic because they may fear offending the person, and also because they may not feel qualified to make a diagnosis and may feel that they are overstepping professional boundaries to even mention it. In general, a therapist who suggests that you may be autistic is worth listening to if they have had several sessions of meeting and speaking with you and so have a good sense of who you are. That is not to say that they are always correct, but their opinion is often valuable as it may highlight something other than, for example, simple depression, which may warrant further investigation.

There Have Been Some Big Changes in My Life, and I Can't Cope Anymore

There are a wide range of life transitions and changes that are often reported as the trigger for initial autism suspicions. It is typically the case that an autistic person creates – consciously or otherwise – a life which fits their capabilities in all aspects – social, sensory, flexibility. This can work perfectly for many years and minimize or avoid all potential causes of challenge or distress for the person, thereby hiding or masking their autistic features. They may live alone or with family, they may eat the same foods every day, watch the same TV programmes, maintain a quiet and ordered home and have limited social interactions with those with shared intense interests, or with no one. It may only be when something changes in the person's life that their struggles with these aspects are revealed.

Leaving home and/or going to university is often one of the first major transitions in adult life, which catches our undiagnosed autistic unawares. Some autistic children excel academically at school and, given that their home environment often accidentally supports their autistic needs – perhaps because there are other (possibly undiagnosed) autistic family members such as parents or siblings who have similar needs – they may have few challenges growing up. It is easy to suppose then that as a young adult they will have little problem adapting to life at university, or living independently elsewhere, and it can be a surprise when this is not the case. For university selection, the focus may be on the course choice and quality of teaching rather than on other aspects of the environment, such as the size of the university, the support available, or the accommodation options. Halls of residence and shared housing are common and may be difficult for an autistic person due to the noise or social requirements. Managing money, preparing food, and keeping up with personal hygiene and self-care may be new experiences previously dealt with by a parent or carer. To do all of these things as well as study in an unfamiliar environment surrounded by unfamiliar people may be the catalyst for burnout, a breakdown, or the onset of mental health issues. It is not uncommon for autistic students to drop out of university for these reasons and others. This overload of triggers can reveal autistic features for the first time, as the person's peers cope fairly easily with this transition to independence in a way that they are unable to. The same can be said for any move away from home into an unfamiliar residence, town, or community. If there are too many changes all at once, it can be hard for an autistic person to assimilate them, and a realization may occur of patterns of difficulty that are not shared with others going through the same experience.

Other transitions which may have a bigger than expected impact for a potentially autistic person are any which similarly result in a new living environment, changes to established routines, sensory changes, or social requirements – new people, more interactions, a new role. You will have learned by now that autistic people can struggle to imagine what a new situation may be like in advance of it happening and may also take considerable time to adjust, if they can adjust at all, to new circumstances, such as:

- First job
- First child
- Moving in with partner
- Moving house
- Changing jobs
- Death of a loved one
- Divorce or end of a relationship

Perimenopause

A much more recent reason given for seeking autism assessment for females is related to perimenopause. For the past few years, our experience has been that the majority of adult females seeking autism assessment are in their 40s and 50s; around the time of perimenopause. They frequently report the same experiences of being exhausted by their efforts to try and work out how to fit in with peers and are tired of masking, pretending to be 'normal', and putting everyone else's needs before their own. The physical aspects of perimenopause may be particularly distressing for autistic people with sensory sensitivities: hot flushes, vertigo, itchy skin, and accompanying mental health changes resulting in increased anxiety, mood swings, and the onset of panic attacks. Insomnia can be a big problem around this time, worsened by night sweats and ruminative, anxious thoughts. Women seeking diagnosis report that their ability to cope with life in the way they did previously has reduced, with some needing to leave their jobs due to brain fog and fatigue, and often wondering if they are losing their mind. A small number of studies have identified similar patterns, and two books due for publication in 2026 focus on the topics of autistic menopause (Moseley and Cobb, 2026). Whilst many of these physical and mental symptoms of perimenopause are common among the entire female population, it may be the case that the hormonal changes associated with this time of life affect autistic women differently. It has been discovered that autistic women are more likely to have polycystic ovary syndrome, which is an endocrine (hormone) based condition, and researchers have found other links between autism and sex hormones (Ingudomnukul et al., 2007; Simantov et al., 2022).

Covid-19

The global Covid-19 pandemic caused a number of people to start to suspect that they were autistic due to their experience of enforced lockdowns, which was a common reason given in that period at assessment interviews for what had led the person to seek assessment. Lockdowns required all members of a family or household to remain at home together for several weeks at a time. Adults did not go to work and children did not go to school, both of which were big changes for most people. The impact of this experience on the mental health of autistic people was often either entirely positive or entirely negative depending on their perspective. Whilst the rest of the world were suffering from social isolation and experiencing increased depression and anxiety, many autistic people had never felt so well. They thrived in a world where social invitations and expectations had disappeared, found online interactions easier due to clear time boundaries, and enjoyed no physical contact and not having to leave their homes. They loved the ability to be in solitude and not be judged for it, to keep to their preferred routines and schedules uninterrupted and to spend hours and hours on their interests. Many found their sensory and mental health difficulties lessened by having to stay at home. The experience revealed to them how exhausted and stressed they had been navigating and traversing the outside world day after day, commuting and interacting and dealing with constant unpredictability, and this led to some suspecting that they might be autistic.

Conversely, the same experience of lockdowns had the opposite effect on others, particularly those with partners and families, who were used to maintaining their own routines, such as time at home whilst the children were at school, or structured time at work and alone time whilst commuting. With the whole family in one place, these periods of alone time and schedules were disrupted, and some people began to realize how heavily they had relied on these familiar routines as a kind of scaffold which enabled them to sustain a sense of normal social and other functioning when required. The removal of these routines resulted in depression, anxiety, and feelings of being totally overwhelmed. For some this was accompanied by guilt at feeling so awful when forced to spend time with their beloved family. Again, thoughts of why their reactions were so extreme led some to consider that they might be autistic. These thoughts were often accompanied by self-reflection on earlier times in their life when they had found similar situations distressing, but had dismissed them at the time.

Alcohol/Drug User – Current or Recovering

Although research is limited in this area, it is not uncommon to see adults seeking assessment who are currently using recreational substances – marijuana and alcohol being the most often cited – as a means of coping with daily life and social interaction. We also see a number of recovering alcoholics and drug users who describe how, since they have been dry or clean, their autistic features have been revealed for the first time. Anecdotally, autistic people report that substances can help with their mental health, in particular anxiety, as they allow them to feel calm and disconnected from a world that is frequently overwhelming. Alcohol is known to be a social lubricant and autistic people say that they are able to tolerate social interactions and communicate more freely after a few drinks. Whilst this is also the case to some extent for all people, this can be taken to the extreme for some autistic people who cannot leave the house without having a drink (or a joint). Rather than simply making social situations a little more relaxed, an autistic person may feel the need to self-medicate for a range of other reasons, for example to cope with everyday changes that most people do not find stressful. They may find that having another person sharing their home and moving or not putting things back in the correct place is too difficult to tolerate. They may find travelling on public transport too overwhelming. Autistic people drink and take drugs for autistic reasons, and taking time to note which occasions are most triggering can be helpful in the autism diagnostic process.

In the book *Asperger Syndrome and Alcohol* (Tinsley and Hendrickx, 2008), Matt Tinsley describes how alcohol allowed him to lead a functioning life of work and relationships by masking his extreme anxiety and making the world, and the people in it, feel less over-stimulating. It was only when, due to his increasing tolerance to alcohol, his consumption was at a level that endangered his life that this became a problem. This type of substance use is defined as a secondary problem, since its purpose is to provide a strategy for managing the primary problem, which for these individuals is undiagnosed autism and the mental challenges that can accompany it. If this is your experience, you will be asked questions in your assessment about how you think and behave without having taken any substances, as this will be a more accurate reflection of your true self and reveal any potential autistic features.

I Saw an Autistic Person on TV/TikTok and They Were Just Like Me

In recent years, mention and portrayal of autism has increased significantly. YouTube and TikTok have given a platform for autistic people to share their experiences and their lives to a worldwide audience and this has led many people to identify with what they see and hear. Caution must be taken, however, about what is created and viewed online, as whilst an autistic person is certainly the expert in their own experience, they are not necessarily in the assessment of autism itself, and there is a lot of misinformation being shared about what constitutes diagnosable features of autism. This has led to some people requesting an autism assessment based on having watched a video online and relating strongly to very specific elements of the narrator's experience, rather than having researched what is required for a full diagnostic autism outcome.

Understandably, these people can sometimes be very disappointed when told that they do not meet the diagnostic criteria, although others may be relieved.

Despite this, fictional portrayals of autism can be very accurate and often lead individuals and/or their family members to remark 'That's just like me/you' and begin a journey of exploration. Matt Tinsley first came across the idea of autism in his 40s when watching a news interview with the author Mark Haddon, whose book *The Curious Incident of the Dog in the Nighttime* (2003) had just been published. Matt recalls hearing the description of the autistic lead character's features and being struck by how many features matched his own. This led to his diagnosis and subsequent recovery from alcoholism. Other fictional characters who show what we may consider to be autistic features, and whom autistic people often relate to, include:

- Sheldon from the TV series *The Big Bang Theory*
- Mr Spock from the TV and film franchise, Star Trek
- Sherlock Holmes from books by Sir Arthur Conan Doyle, also in TV and films
- Saga Noren from Swedish/Danish TV series *The Bridge*
- Sam from TV series, *Atypical*
- Christian Wolff from the movie *The Accountant*
- Max Braverman from TV series *Parenthood*
- Woo Young-woo from South Korean TV series *Extraordinary Attorney Woo*

Fictional representations of autism tend to be somewhat intensified and extreme as this makes for interesting viewing, but it can lead to thoughts of 'I can't be autistic because I don't do that'. Most autistic people do not present their autistic features in such stereotypical and visually obvious ways; for example, they don't all do endless calculations in their heads and offend people every time they open their mouths. Whilst these presentations of autism are very helpful in raising awareness and expanding the audience of people educated in autism, it can lead to unrealistic representations, which may deter some from seeking assessment because they perceive that autism has a more extreme presentation than their own. Given that most autistic adults have learned how to behave in a socially acceptable manner through masking and conscious learning, relying on fictional autistic characters is only partially helpful.

Other real-life well-known people have also disclosed their autism diagnoses, and some people relate to their characteristics and experiences:

- Chris Packham, UK naturalist and TV presenter
- Greta Thunberg, Swedish environmental activist
- Susan Boyle, Scottish singer
- Dan Ackroyd, US actor
- Daryl Hannah, US actor
- Anthony Hopkins, UK actor
- Satoshi Tajiri, Japanese creator of the Pokémon franchise

Whilst relating to individual aspects of an autistic person's experience can certainly mean a higher likelihood of being autistic yourself, the diagnostic process requires all of the criteria to be met above a certain threshold and across the lifespan. If you do find yourself seeing great similarities between yourself and an autistic fictional character, try and think about what exactly those features are that you see in yourself. Are they very precise in their language? Do they have intense interests? Are they socially uncomfortable with typical eye contact?

What is important to note is that none of the above responses or thought processes in themselves mean that someone is autistic. As well as these initial triggering events that sparked the idea of autism as a possibility, it is necessary to think about whether there were other signs in childhood or patterns that have emerged throughout life that also indicate possible autistic features.

If you were in an autism assessment interview and were asked the question 'What brings you here?', how would you respond? What is the journey that you have taken from first learning about autism to this point?

Self-Assessment for Chapter 3 –
Reasons for Considering Autism

Make some notes on the pages at the back of the book about your reasons for considering autism at this time in your life.

Do your reasons for suspecting autism resonate
with those listed?   ☐ Yes ☐ No

Score yourself between 0 and 10 on the likelihood that you are autistic:

. . . .

Chapter 4

I Can't Be Autistic Because...

So, you've got this far in your investigation to determine whether you might be autistic. You've read the diagnostic criteria and a few, or many, bells have rung, light bulbs have gone off, and several other metaphors to describe a sense of relating and resonating with what you have read. But... there is this other niggly stuff that doesn't quite fit; some of your characteristics, experiences, and behaviours that sit squarely in the 'Reasons I Am Not Autistic' column on your 'Am I Autistic?' spreadsheet/list. If you don't have a spreadsheet or a list, you should write that in the 'Not Autistic' column, only you can't because you don't have one.

In this chapter, we seek to dispel some of the common features that people often give as reasons that they 'can't be autistic', but which usually do not actually offer any evidence of the sort. It may be that you have been told that you can't be autistic by a medical, or other, professional, family member, friend, or anyone else who either is or feels qualified to offer an opinion on these matters (often based on scant knowledge of your experiences). It may be your own perception of what autism 'should look like' based on media portrayals such as Rain Man. It is amazing what a strong impact that film had on views of autism, and continues to have, given that it was made in 1988 and much has changed since then. It may be that you have already unknowingly met autistic children, or that your own knowledge of autism is actually pretty basic or fundamentally wrong, without being aware of it.

We shall take a look at each of a number of these beliefs and explain how they make no bearing whatsoever on your potential autistic status. It may well be the case that autistic people can, for example, make eye contact, have children, and work a job, but none of these individually would be a reason to assess a person as not autistic. What is more important is the length of the 'Reasons I am Autistic' list – as long as the features on that list are actually diagnostic autistic features and not those gleaned from often unreliable social media.

It's also worth mentioning that if your 'Reasons I Am Autistic' list is quite long, and the 'Not Autistic' list is much shorter, then one tiny, missed autistic diagnostic characteristic does not override all of the others that meet the criteria. That is called black-and-white thinking and should be on the 'Reasons I Am Autistic' list.

We offer no judgement here about being 'normal' or how you should behave. We seek to explain why your beliefs about yourself may or may not fit within commonly accepted behaviours.

I Can Make Eye Contact

Whilst the expression and interpretation of non-verbal social communication gestures such as facial expressions and body language are a key component to the diagnostic criteria for autism, and eye contact is mentioned in both the ICD-11 and the DSM-5, this is only given as an example of possible behaviours that may be seen and is not obligatory.

Eye contact consists of both ends of the eye gaze spectrum, encompassing non-existent or limited gaze through to constant gaze, or staring.

It is entirely possible that you can make perfectly culturally typical eye contact and be autistic. It is also the case that you may actually have differences in your eye contact which do meet the diagnostic criteria, but perhaps haven't considered them in that way because you assume that everyone else is engaging in the same processes as you are.

If you are constantly aware that you are consciously monitoring your eye contact in an effortful and possibly tiring way, then it may be that your innate level of ease in making eye contact in a way that is culturally accepted is atypical.

If you feel that you have 'learned' to make eye contact, then this is atypical. Most people do not have to learn how to do it, or even give it much thought, ever.

If, when you think about it, you don't actually look at people's eyes at all, and instead look at mouths, noses, foreheads, or over shoulders, this would also be considered atypical. Most non-autistic people do not consciously think about their own eye contact at all. It is entirely intuitive and without discomfort in all but the most rare situations.

I Would Have Been Diagnosed by Now

Many people state that the reason that they cannot possibly be autistic is that someone would have spotted it by now and diagnosed them. Whilst this may have been true if your autistic characteristics were very clear and troublesome to either you or those taking care of you at a young age, for most autistic people, this is not the case. Even if it were, the premise also assumes that those within the sphere of your childhood autistic self had some knowledge of autism; the further back you were born, the less likely this would have been. Also, given the genetic nature of autism, the likelihood is that the potentially autistic person reading this book (that's you, by the way) was not the only autistic person in the household when you were growing up. What this means is that your home life may have accidentally been very 'autism-friendly': structured, routine-driven, repetitious, environmentally gentle, and low on spontaneous social activities. All of which could result in an upbringing that didn't feel very stressful at all, and which didn't trigger frequent bouts of obvious autistic distress, which may have alerted your caregivers and educators.

Some autistic children love school (although many don't) – or should we say that they love the classroom. These children enjoy the structure, the rules, the hierarchy, and the clearly stated expectations.

They often don't love the playground, which offers none of the above. Again, these clearly defined rules and boundaries of the classroom may mean that your autisticness did not reveal itself.

It is also not necessarily the case that you would have been diagnosed by now if you do not have any intellectual disability, had no delays in your development as a child, you were born before 1994, and/or you were not assigned male at birth. It will also depend enormously on the country that you grew up in and the knowledge, resources, and availability of diagnosis there.

Until the mid-90s, autism was considered to be rare, mainly affecting males and only those with intellectual disabilities and/or those with late development, particularly in speech. This means that if you did not meet any of the above criteria as a child, you would have been unlikely to have come to the attention of medical professionals who could have referred you for diagnosis. Asperger syndrome was introduced into the diagnostic manuals in around 1994 and the criteria for this subcategory of autism specified that no language delay and no intellectual disability could be present, but that all other features of autism must be met. This was the first time that anyone with average or high intelligence could be diagnosed as autistic. Asperger syndrome as a named subcategory was removed from diagnostic manuals in 2015 along with 'High Functioning Autism' and 'Classic Autism', to be replaced by a more general 'Autism Spectrum Disorder' diagnosis. Further identification of levels of support are now indicated by the severity levels 1–3, as outlined in Chapter 1.

In current times, with the increasing realization that autism is more common than originally thought, is largely genetic/inherited, and is present in individuals across the entire range of intellectual ability, it is very common that a person may not have considered they could be autistic until recently – well into their adult life. We have seen people in their 80s coming forward for diagnosis, saying that they just want to know who they are, demonstrating that there can be value in diagnosis at any age.

The first introduction to autism for many people is through the diagnosis of a child within the family. Today, child diagnosis is increasingly available in a way that it wasn't for those who are now older adults, which explains how higher numbers of autistic children are now being identified than in the past. Adult relatives may be present during the child's assessment, undertake research or reflect on their own childhood in light of the diagnosis, and realize that the diagnosed child is 'just like me'. This can be a revelatory moment met with relief, sadness, and/or denial.

If you are of average or above average intellectual ability, you are likely to have 'flown under the radar' of any possible suspicion of your being autistic as a child, since again, there may not have been any 'problem' which drew attention to you for being different or 'difficult'. Adult diagnosed autistic people often state that they were quiet and well-behaved, often liked by their teachers for their mature manner and adherence to the rules, displaying behaviours which gave no cause for concern. In the case of accompanying ADHD features, the child may well have been considered as just 'naughty' and the autism may have been missed. The sensory and social demands as well as the uncertainty of the school environment can cause great distress to some autistic children, but this is often attributed simply to being an anxious child, rather than considering any underlying cause.

Anecdotally, we also see that fewer people from lower socioeconomic backgrounds are accessing diagnosis, suggesting that for a number of reasons, including education and financial resources, that those from this group may be disproportionately undiagnosed.

The prevalence of females and non-binary people within the autistic population has been significantly underestimated throughout autism's modern history up until around 2013. Despite many lived-experience books being written by autistic women, such as Professor Temple Grandin and Donna Williams, the general consensus among medical professionals, educators, and the general public was that autism was predominantly a male phenomenon. Even if a girl presented clear autistic features, she was more likely to be given a diagnosis of a psychological condition such as an anxiety disorder, obsessive-compulsive disorder (OCD), emotionally unstable personality disorder (EUPD), or borderline personality disorder (BPD). Sadly, this remains the case even among adults, and many females seeking autism diagnosis arrive at the assessment with a long list of previous mental health diagnoses, none of which they believe 'quite fit' their profile and experience. The first conferences and training courses focused on female experience of autism only took place around 2014, and in the literature review of the first edition of the book *Women and Girls on the Autism Spectrum* (Hendrickx, 2014) there were only around 20 research papers on autism in existence which mentioned gender at all. Therefore, if you were assigned female at birth, the chance of you having been diagnosed as autistic as a child, or even as an adult, are extremely small.

The breadth of knowledge and expertise on autism varies widely across the globe and the availability of up-to-date, accurate autism assessment is also extremely location dependent. As a general overview, our experience is that the UK and countries in Northern Europe are leading the field on autism research and that most of it is in English. Many of these countries have state-funded healthcare systems which may facilitate access to assessment. The USA appears to be less prolific in research and availability of diagnosis, perhaps partially due to their lack of state-funded healthcare. Other parts of the globe offer variable understanding and access. Our experience is that many individuals from countries around the world who seek assessment via services that we work for or run, which are based in the UK, tell us that assessment is very difficult to obtain and that understanding of autism in adults/females/non-intellectually disabled people is often non-existent. Therefore, if you hail from outside of Europe or the US, your opportunities for being spotted as possibly autistic are very slim.

So, in summary, although with less frequency than in the past, all of the above reasons for missed diagnosis and misdiagnosis still occur; it is therefore definitely not the case that you would have been diagnosed by now, especially if one or more of the above factors applies to you.

I Have a Job

The list of brilliant people suspected of being autistic is long and includes Albert Einstein, Steve Jobs, and Bill Gates, all of whom definitely had jobs and were very good at them. In our experience, most people that seek adult autism assessment are employed, many successfully so. The reasons that autistic people find working difficult is often due to factors related to dealing with people, rules that don't make any sense, and overwhelming physical environments. Office politics and assumed hierarchy can be problematic as this means working out when someone is taking advantage of you, and whether it is OK to tell your boss that they are an idiot. Autistic people can also find working in teams challenging due to needing to take on board the views of others, communicate tactfully, and compromise, all of which can be highly effortful. Fast-paced and changing priorities, interruptions, and loose adherence to rules often upset autistic people and they are maybe the only ones who read the employee handbook and actually stick to its procedures and guidance, foolishly expecting everyone else to be doing the same. Sensory factors such as tolerating a commute on public transport with its lights, noise, smells, and proximity issues followed by eight hours in an office, factory, or other setting full of more of the same can take its toll.

Despite all of these factors, most autistic people manage to tolerate it and sustain employment. Some have found a workplace that suits them socially, mentally, and environmentally and they just stay there for decades, happily repeating the same tasks – which may involve their deep interests – in the same environment, with the same people. The concept of career progression is alien to some autistic people who just want to do what they love whilst not being uncomfortable. For others, their employment history and CV may be of considerable length as they find multiple workplaces to be intolerable for one reason or another (generally related to autism-derived challenges) and leave/get fired and start over again. A diagnosis of autism can be revelatory in solving the puzzle of why someone has failed to find tolerable employment despite being qualified, smart, and capable.

For autistic people who have found success in their working life, we see patterns in their choices. They are generally involved in an industry or field that they have an intense interest in and passion for. This can be anything from fashion, to science, to working with trains, to knitting and 18th century art. The aspects of work that seem to appeal to autistic people involve knowledge, data, repetition, patterns, and solving problems. Computing, accounting, psychology, forensics, crafts, proofreading, writing, teaching, science, and medicine are just a few. A reported 1% of doctors, primarily GPs and psychiatrists, are autistic (Doherty et al., 2021) and GCHQ, the UK Government Communication Headquarters, have actively sought neurodiverse employees for roles in cybersecurity for their 'fast pattern recognition, sharper accuracy and greater attention to detail' (Jolly, 2022) – skills which are equally useful in knitting and as a therapist.

There appear to be quite a number of autistic people who are self-employed and run their own businesses. The absence of management can allow for choices to be made about working hours, social interactions, time management, and working environment, thereby removing or reducing all of the challenges of a standard workplace. Working part-time, from home, and alone all feature as protective factors for autistic people in employment, and the post-Covid world has proved highly advantageous to those autistic people whose employment has changed as a result.

Whilst many autistic people do work, this can come at a cost which typically relates to physical and mental health. Autistic burnout is a frequently repeated occurrence along with anxiety and depression, which can be caused by many factors relating to the job itself, the people, the values of the organization, or the sensory environment. So, whilst an autistic person may have a job, they may find it a heavier load than their peers and colleagues.

So there we have it. Having a job certainly does not preclude a person from being autistic. In fact, being good at certain jobs, or having the specific skills that are required to do them well, may actually be an increased indicator of autism.

I Have Children

The idea that autistic people are not capable of having a successful relationship and parenting children is illogical and nonsense. Autistic people make both good and bad parents, just like anyone else. Some autistic people have no interest at all in having children, and others make it their special interest and life's purpose, having large numbers of kids. Some autistic adults find children (and animals) far easier to get along with than adults as they are less judgemental and more forgiving of perceived social tactlessness and awkwardness, permitting an acceptance of the autistic person's idiosyncratic behaviours. This means that they can be found playing with them at social events, rather than conversing with the adults like everyone else in attendance. Having said that, some autistic adults find children utterly terrifying because they are expected to anticipate the child's needs, prioritize them over their own, and take responsibility for the physical and emotional safety of another human being. Children can be less predictable and more emotional than adults and this can create an additional level of uncertainty for an autistic person.

Additionally, autism is an inherited/genetic condition and in order for it to be perpetuated, it must be passed down through generations, and that means sexual relationships with individuals of different sexes. It is therefore likely that one or both of your parents is/was autistic as were their ancestors before them. It is equally likely that one or more of your children will present with autistic features, and their future children too, and so on...

Having children, wanting to have children, not wanting children, hating children, or liking children has no bearing on the likelihood of you being autistic.

I Am an Extrovert, I Like People, and I Have Friends

Whilst it is often the case that autistic people find neurotypical people exhausting, confusing, complicated, scary, stupid, unpredictable, pointless, dishonest, and many other things, it is usually the case that most autistic people like at least one being in the world, even if that is their dog.

There is nothing within the diagnostic criteria that says that autistic people are introverted, and this is certainly not the case. Some autistic people are highly social and love to go out and talk to people. It should be noted that this social behaviour would still fit within the diagnostic criteria, and so may be less reciprocal in nature than neurotypical interactions and perhaps less frequent, requiring rehearsal and preparation beforehand and recovery time afterwards. It may be only with a very small number of known people and/or solely focused on a singular topic of interest or hobby, such as Harry Potter, football, or serial killers (all popular autistic choices) rather than general chat about shoes, holidays, and what you did at the weekend, unless these events involve any of the above topics of interest.

Autistic people tend to find other neurodivergent people much easier to get along with, and often feel less judged by their own community. When thinking back on childhood friendships, if there were any, most autistic people identify that they gravitated unknowingly towards similar souls. There is an unspoken level of understanding among autistic people that 'whilst I might not be quite your brand of weird, I can respect its presence and I am not threatened in any way by it'. Autistic people very frequently report that neurotypical people show disapproval, rejection and judgement for their ways of thinking and being, which leads to masking behaviours, anxiety, low self-esteem, and avoidance of social interactions.

A general statement which perhaps sums up the autistic perspective on social interaction is that 'I like to spend a specific amount of time with specific people doing a specific activity. My way, my people, my terms'. They are just more selective about who, what, and how they spend their time than most people due to the effort required to say and do the right thing, how quickly their social battery runs down, and how long it takes to recover.

I Have a Sense of Humour

It can certainly seem like a requirement to have a sense of humour as an autistic person in a non-autistic world. There is mention in the diagnostic criteria about differences in understanding language and communication, particularly that which is incongruous, vague, or at odds with the meaning or context of the situation, such as jokes, sarcasm, hidden agendas, and lies. It is called 'receptive' language when a person is on the receiving end of the communication. There is, however, no mention of any challenges in 'expressive' language, which is the production of this type of language by an autistic person and there are a number of highly successful autistic stand-up comedians, including Pierre Novellie, author of *Why Can't I Just Enjoy Things?* (2024), Fern Brady, author of *Strong Female Character* (2023), and multi-award-winning comedian Hannah Gadsby.

Autistic people are often highly observant, aware of the illogical differences between their own thoughts and behaviours and that of those around them, and can find this funny. They can also communicate these observations using precise and straightforward language, which others may find shocking, which is funny. When these anomalies and inconsistencies are pointed out to the neurotypical population who generated them via comedy, the audience can also identify with these observations and also find them funny. Weirdly, it doesn't stop them doing them though. Sigh.

I Don't Line Things Up

You don't have to line things up to be autistic, but you might order, sequence, categorize, straighten, systemize, collect, align, place, and arrange things. This ordering may be by colour, size, occasion, or genre, alphabetically, chronologically, or any other criteria that you can think of. These things may be ordinary everyday things, such as tins, books, toy cars, teddies, pens, towels, the remote control, peas, perfume bottles, fruit, or socks. Take a look in your kitchen cupboards or pants drawer and see if placement and order is important to you. A repeated use of spreadsheets to collect, collate, and order data on a wide range of daily tasks, such as extensive meal plans, chore rotas, a list of every movie you have ever watched, numbers of socks etc. all counts as 'lining up'. You may not have considered that you even do anything unusual with these items, but look closely and ask yourself what your reaction is when you find that one of these items has been moved or changed. That may tell you how important order is to you.

I'm Not Obsessed with Trains/Dinosaurs/Horses

Whilst the diagnostic criteria do specify repetition and intensity in interests, the subject of an autistic person's interests are irrelevant – it is the all-consuming nature and depth of knowledge and passion for it that matters. Historically, in the male-child-only understanding of autism, trains and dinosaurs would perhaps have been common interests, but those were the days before Pokémon, Harry Potter, Minecraft, and Taylor Swift, which we would postulate as taking top spots on the autism interest list these days. For adults, the same topics of interest may well remain, with some autistic people making careers out of their childhood fascinations, sometimes becoming world-class experts in their field. More commonly, autistic interests change throughout the lifespan, and trains may be replaced by mountain bikes, Renaissance art, cooking, cross-stitch, serial killers, *Friends*, lamp posts, frogs, or any other single thing that you can imagine. For autistic people, the interest often ends when the initial steep learning phase plateaus (I have researched all the kettles, I know every breed of cat), when it is completed (the marathon has been run, I have bought the new kettle/cat), or where further progress is not practically possible (finances, location etc.). This can differ from those with ADHD whose initial dopamine-inspired interest wanes almost as soon as the first parcel of purchased equipment arrives in the post and depth or completion are rarely achieved.

Anything counts if it is your whole world, even if only for a relevantly short period of time – and you don't need to know a single fact about velociraptors.

I Don't Mind My Food Touching

As with lining things up, the placement of food items on a plate is important to many autistic people, particularly in their childhoods – many autistic adults appear to cope much better without a chip barrier or their baked beans in a separate pot later in life. The rationale behind this is twofold. One is about avoiding the contamination of different food items with each other, the result of which would change the appearance, texture, and flavour of each. For example, baked beans on toast is an entirely different gustatory experience than toast and baked beans consumed individually, and that would be wrong.

Second, as with any other possession or object, there may be a visually 'right' place for it to be on a plate, and the separation of items – which avoids the blurring of their placement – may be essential. The black-and-white thinking facet of autism is often very clear about what is 'right' and what is 'wrong', even when it comes to where the ketchup is placed on the plate.

And just when it all seemed so clear, some autistic people like to mash all items of their food up into one big pile so that the appearance, texture, and taste are consistent throughout. The behaviour is different, but the outcome remains the same: certainty.

All that being said, it is not a requirement of autism for you to experience distress at a stray pea infiltrating the mashed potato camp, but if you can tolerate baked beans and fried eggs on the same plate, you are simply a monster.

I Am Empathic

Ah, now this is a touchy subject for many autistic people, as historically the idea that they do not have empathy has been key to the diagnosis, which has put autistic people into the same camp as psychopaths, serial killers, and other less-than-pleasant humans. It is reasonable therefore that some autistic people may object to this idea on this basis alone. It is also the case that many autistic people do feel and mirror the emotions of others extremely strongly, and struggle to differentiate others' emotions from their own, sometimes to the detriment of their own well-being. Other autistic people state that they have no clue whatsoever what anyone else is thinking or feeling and if they see someone crying, will hope and pray that someone else deals with them so that they don't have to. Clearly then, there has been some misunderstanding about this 'empathy' word and what it really means for autistic people.

Several different types of empathy are thought to exist in varying degrees across the population, so it's not as simple as either having it or not. Cognitive empathy is where you can understand what another person is feeling. Affective empathy involves actually physically feeling that person's emotions. And compassionate empathy is where you are driven to spontaneously offer assistance. Added to this for autistic people is the concept of *The Double Empathy Problem* (Milton, 2012), mentioned previously, which suggests that there can be a mismatch between the communication and social styles of autistic and non-autistic people and that this can cause mutual difficulties with identifying and understanding how each other feels. The autistic and non-autistic experience differs in terms of social experience, sensory experience, values, and priorities, and so it would be reasonable to expect that each would find it hard to understand why something might matter so much to the other when it doesn't matter to them. It appears to be the case that autistic people can often do this with other autistic people, but less so with non-autistic people. The same applies to the non-autistic population, hence the development of the belief that autistic people do not have empathy, when in fact it is that each group struggles to empathize with the other whilst finding it instinctively easier to do so within their own. The Embrace Autism website has a great article which explains this in a little more detail and gives some excellent examples of different types of empathy in action (Silvertant, 2023).

It is important to note that the empathy profile of a psychopath is very different to that of an autistic person, so even you are somewhat lost when faced with the emotions of another person (potentially autistic), this does not mean that the idea of causing them deliberate harm or chopping them up into small pieces sounds like fun (potentially psychopathic).

In summary, having empathy doesn't preclude the possibility that you may be autistic.

I Am Not Good at Maths/Science

It is likely that the myth that autistic people have high mathematical or scientific ability stems from the now outdated belief that autism is more prevalent in males. The fields of maths, science, technology, and engineering are dominated by men academically and profession-ally, and the stereotyped 'geek' lives on in these worlds. The autis-tic way of thinking is considered diagnostically to be linear, black and white, and certainty seeking, seen in the lining up of toys, data gathering, adherence to rules and enjoyment of repetition. For some autistic people, words and language are their superpower. Language, like maths, also has rules, patterns, repetition, and can be studied both academically and socially. Learning foreign languages comes easily for some autistic people who may be able to speak numerous languages, and are intensely interested in doing so despite the social challenges of actually using them in real life. We may think that words are not our friends as autistic people because of their associa-tion with communication, social interaction, and general confusion (when people don't say what they mean), but this is not always the case. It is also not necessary to be a literary genius to be autistic; you can just be average at either maths or language, or even entirely clue-less at both. It matters not, neither is a factor in itself as to whether a person is autistic or not.

Only Boys Get Autism, and I'm Not One

As mentioned previously, the realization that autism may be as prevalent in non-males (females and others) as in males has been relatively recent. Our former understanding of autism was based on the research of Kanner and Asperger, which only studied boys – being both male and children – and this resulted in a long his-tory of a very narrow profile of what autism may look like, which mainly excluded adults and females. This view has now been soundly smashed to pieces, and a much broader understanding of autism across all ages and genders has replaced it. There is much talk of a 'female autistic profile', which seeks to describe how some autistic women have sought to use their logical autistic cognitive thinking style to analyse the neurotypical human behaviour that they may not fully intuitively understand. After all, it is no coincidence that many autistic people describe feeling like an 'alien' or on the 'wrong planet' for many years prior to diagnosis. This analysis results in the creation of rules, scripts, and personas with which the autistic person attempts to assimilate, camouflage, or mask their way through life to try to fit in and appear 'normal' and/or invisible. We now know that these behaviours can come at a great cost mentally and physically, and that they are not unique to females. Being female is no barrier to being autistic, in fact being female and adult probably means that you had less chance of being diagnosed as a child and therefore it's more likely that you remain undiagnosed now.

I Don't Have Routines/Rituals

We bet you do. We would suggest that the majority of all people have their own little preferences and rules about how they live life, so having none at all would be unusual. However, when considering autistic behaviours from a stereotypical perspective, you may expect that autistic people lead their daily lives in an extremely rigid and repetitive fashion, and many do, but not all. It is true that the diagnostic elements require an insistence on sameness and an inflexible adherence to routines (APA, 2013), but how these manifest can vary widely between individuals. For some, there is a requirement for a fixed schedule and plan for all events and activities, which cannot be changed. For others, repetition and sameness – in meals, clothes, activities, products, books, movies, and conversation are paramount. Typically, autistic people are not big fans of surprises and spontaneity and like to know what's coming. In essence, autism is about seeking certainty – in 'knowing', whether that be information on a topic, predicting what will happen when, or choosing the same meal in the same restaurant because every aspect of it will be exactly the same as it was last time. This slightly less literal definition of 'routine' as 'certainty seeking' can broaden our awareness of what counts according to the diagnostic criteria. It is also the case that some autistic people have elected – by choice or necessity, but sometimes without realizing it – to live lives which limit uncertainty, resulting in little discomfort, and may therefore not recognize that they are as routine-driven as they actually are. They may only engage in a limited range of activities, remain at home where they are less likely to encounter unexpected events, stay in the same job for decades, and limit their interactions with people, who are the biggest culprits of uncertainty. It is only by examining many aspects of your life that you can really ascertain whether you are in fact more driven by sameness than by novelty. So, whilst this general characteristic of certainty seeking is required for diagnosis, it may show itself in a whole variety of ways which are more rigid than they may first appear.

I Like Change and I'm Really Spontaneous

Autistic people can love change, but only if it was their idea. The reason being that at the point of instigating the change, the autistic person has done all of their research, mitigated as many possible snags as they can, rationalized the need for the change, and assimilated the new situation into their very being, at which point it becomes easy. Autistic people can travel widely, take up new sports and interests, and start eating brand new foods. From the outside, this can look rather flexible, and even impulsive at times, but this is rarely the case. Great mental effort will likely have taken place to carry out all of the aforementioned tasks, perhaps over many days or months, before the leap takes place.

Change imposed by other people, on the spot and out of the blue, however, is a whole different thing and likely to cause great anxiety, distress, anger, and/or confusion, although none of this may be visible or evident (see masking). Unexpected change may take the form of a loud bang, a question, an interruption, a late change, a new label on a jar of jam, a touch, and many millions of other everyday events, each one of which was not asked for, anticipated, or welcome. This is the change that gives autistic people a bad name and reveals their differences when their reactions to said change is considered inappropriate or disproportionate to the situation by other people. So, if you feel yourself to be untroubled by change, consider whether there is any differentiation between who instigates the change and whether you have subconsciously (or not) created a life which doesn't leave much room for much to surprise you.

In summary then, we cannot think of any one individual human feature that would exclude a person from being autistic. Not one. So, if on your quest to discover whether you are indeed autistic, you have gathered numerous reasons and characteristics which suggest that you might be, then there is not any singular feature that will override all of those and render them null and void. Your quest continues...

Self-Assessment for Chapter 4 – Reasons Why I Can't Be Autistic

Make some notes about any existing reasons that you believe mean that you cannot be autistic. Do they correspond with any of the above? Try to research whether they come from you having an outdated or uninformed view of how autism might present. List any further reasons which remain valid.

Have your reasons why you can't be autistic
been explained?   ☐ Yes ☐ No

Score yourself between 0 and 10 on the likelihood that you are autistic:

. . . .

Chapter 5

Supporting Evidence

CO-OCCURRING CONDITIONS AND OTHER FACTORS
WHICH MAY SUPPORT THE LIKELIHOOD OF AUTISM

The aim of this chapter is not to diagnose any of these conditions but to give an overview of the most commonly recognized co-occurring conditions and other factors that are seen alongside autism. If you have one or more of the following conditions/additional factors it does not necessarily mean that you are autistic, and if you have none it doesn't mean you are not. However, there does appear to be elevated rates of autistic people with something else going on, and it can be useful additional information when seeking a diagnosis.

It is commonly understood that a lot of autistic people also have co-occurring conditions affecting their physical and mental health, including other neurodevelopmental conditions. For some people, diagnosis of related conditions comes before they have even considered the idea of autism. A number of conditions which also affect people physically, such as polycystic ovary syndrome (PCOS), chronic fatigue syndrome (CFS) or myalgic encephalomyelitis (ME), fibromyalgia, Ehlers-Danlos syndrome, and irritable bowel syndrome (IBS), appear to have a link to autism, but at the time of writing, only small amounts of research have been carried out. We also mention gender identity, sexuality, and family medical history which are also possible supporting factors.

Alexithymia

Alexithymia or 'emotional blindness' is a difficulty in deciphering how you feel emotionally. People who experience alexithymia may have a basic understanding of how they feel when they are happy, sad, angry, or anxious, but may struggle with more nuanced emotions such as insecure, accepted, or vulnerable. They may be able to interpret or express their feelings eventually, but to do so may take a lot of mental work and/or time to mechanically figure out what has happened and the impact that may have had. It may also be that if someone treats you badly or something terrible happens, you may not react at all at the time, making it appear that you don't care or have accepted how you were treated. It may be some time later that you have a strong emotional reaction, almost as though your brain needed time to catch up emotionally. If you have ever carried out an internet search to figure out what or why you are feeling a certain way, this may be an indication to look into alexithymia deeper. Furthermore, people with alexithymia may also react emotionally to situations differently, laughing when being told someone has died, or crying for no apparent reason.

Alexithymia appears to be common in the autistic population, and even though the exact percentage is hard to settle on, researchers believe it could be anywhere between 50 and 85% (Wilkinson, 2017). As this figure shows, it is not universal within the autistic population and, even though the figures are high, it is not part of the diagnostic criteria. Anecdotally, many people do not even realize that their struggle in being able to know how they feel is atypical, especially when younger.

There is a test that can be taken online that measures alexithymia called the Toronto Alexithymia Scale, which is listed in the Resources section at the back of the book.

Anxiety

It is a well-reported fact that the majority of autistic people live with underlying anxiety on a daily basis, even if they have not been clinically diagnosed. A good practice guide for mental health professionals published by the National Autistic Society (NAS, 2021) found that 94% of the adult participants surveyed experience anxiety.

Anxiety can be brought on by many different situations for autistic people, but especially those that include social interactions, new situations or environments, or change. This is not really surprising if you think about the challenges a neuronormative world poses to autistic people. When people are out of their safe space at home, the environment tends to be loud, bright, and smelly for the most part. If you add in a requirement to interact with people, a dose of imposed change and unpredictability, it's no wonder most autistic people feel anxious.

Anxiety presents itself differently, for different people, and in different situations. It can be anything from a slight flutter in the stomach to full-on feelings of panic; from slightly clammy hands to a whole body dripping with sweat. Not everyone is aware that they experience what is termed anxiety, as their sensations are their version of normal, and they may assume that everyone else feels the same way that they do.

Autistic people may have been previously diagnosed with an anxiety disorder, or they may have no diagnosis whatsoever, but know that they live with an uncomfortable level of worry, stress, or fear on a daily basis, all of which come under the umbrella of anxiety. If this is the case, an anxiety diary could provide information and a means of learning what affects you the most. There are many ways that you could go about this but here are some key points that would be helpful to record:

- The date
- Where you were – was it a new or familiar place
- What you were doing
- At which point did your anxiety peak – before, during, or after the event – and for how long did it last
- Consider what the environment was like including any sensory input
- Give your anxiety a level – whatever scale works for you (0–10, a colour key)

Once you have identified what triggers the peaks in anxiety, you can then think about how to manage or overcome some of your anxiety, if you feel able. There are many theories and approaches to doing this, both alone or with the support of a therapist or someone close to you, which are beyond the scope of this book. Huge changes can be made, but, if you are autistic the methods used must be from an autistic understanding and basepoint. The autistic experience of the world is different from that of the general population, and any support must reflect this.

Depression

Just like anxiety, depression is also common in autistic people. Some people diagnosed with depression can have what is described as 'treatment resistant depression' where the person does not respond to two or more different treatment approaches. Some autistic people have been diagnosed with depression, but following diagnosis realized that they had never actually been depressed, but were simply struggling due to finding everyday life hard and this had looked like depression. Depression is more than just feeling low for a few days, and people cannot just snap out of it by exercising or being more social. There are many triggers for depression including big life-changing events such as a break-up, bereavement, or losing your job. Anecdotally, autistic people describe feeling like they do not fit in or are looking at the world from the outside, which can contribute to depression as well. As the world does not tend to be as accessible for the majority of autistic people, that can lead to isolation and finding life too much to cope with. Autistic people may also be predisposed to depression if a family member has experienced it at some point in their life.

Post-natal depression also appears more common in autistic mothers than the general population, with one study finding 58% of autistic mothers had suffered with post-natal depression (Pohl et al., 2020, p. 10). In the same study, autistic mothers reported feeling more isolated, having difficulties communicating with professionals, and struggling with juggling all aspects of new parenthood compared to non-autistic mothers. These, along with a fear of getting it wrong and how others perceive their parenting skills, could be factors for autistic women to develop post-natal depression. It is widely discussed among autistic women, with and without children, how hard they find it to seek help from doctors at the best of times, let alone when they feel like they haven't slept in an eternity and like they can't cope.

If you feel that you have depression, seek help, either from those around you or medical professionals.

Eating Differences

The three most common eating disorders associated with autism are anorexia nervosa, avoidant restrictive food intake disorder (ARFID), and pica. The majority of research on these conditions tends to be focused on females with anorexia, or restrictive eating patterns in children.

Eating differences within the autistic population can present first at any point throughout someone's life, and may last throughout their lives or for a short period of time. If you have had any eating differences, past or present, it is important to note these in any supporting documentation.

General Eating Differences – Non-Clinical

Autistic people's relationship with food and drink does appear to differ to that of the neurotypical population. Even if you do not have or have never had a clinical eating disorder, it is worthwhile noting your experiences with food and drink. You may have noticed this is due to seeking or avoiding different foods due to the sensory aspect (taste and texture), any fixed routines you have around eating/drinking (times, same meals on a daily basis, only being able to have a drink from a certain mug), or difficulties with planning and executing meals. Eating is something that has to be done, multiple times per day, every day for as long as you live. Some autistic people would like to just be able to take a pill three times per day to fulfil all of their nutritional needs.

Anorexia nervosa

People with anorexia restrict the intake of food to the point where they reach a dangerously low weight. The motivations behind this may be different for autistic people. Many people believe that anorexia is driven by body dysmorphia (seeing your body differently from how it actually is) and feeling a need to change it. However, there is an understanding that for autistic people, the weight loss may be the result of needing to have a very set but limited number of calories per day, having to do extensive exercise, a very strict routine around what the person can and cannot eat, or feeling that they cannot be over a certain weight. This is not to dismiss that for some body dysmorphia is the cause or at least plays a role, but this hopefully gives an idea that it is not always the case.

There are links between autism and anorexia, with some studies suggesting that up to 37% of anorexic patients are also autistic (Adamson et al., 2022, p. 592). More research has been done in recent years on the overlaps and best course of treatment for autistic anorexic patients. There now appears to be a better understanding that traditional therapies and treatment plans are not always the best path for a patient who is also autistic. Many of the existing treatments include group work, which is something that can be a barrier for autistic individuals, as well as the overwhelming sensory nature of in-patient units.

ARFID

ARFID is not just being a 'picky eater', being on a fad diet, or choosing not to eat items due to cultural or religious reasons. People with ARFID eat a very limited range of foods and the reasons for this will vary. They may include, but are not limited to, an aversion to the sensory experience of eating particular foods (taste and texture), having little to no interest in food (it getting in the way of fun activities), or being concerned about what will happen if you eat certain foods (for example, vomiting/upset stomach). Having such a restrictive diet can cause weight loss but this is not the motivation for it.

Pica

People with pica have a compulsion to eat non-food items, which are either non-edible or non-nutritious. There is a suggestion that autistic people with pica engage in this for the sensory aspect, which is certainly something that is reported when assessing people for autism. The sensory nature of most items that are consumed, like sponge, rubber, plastic bricks, glass, or crayons, cannot be replicated by edible food items. If these items are swallowed they can be very detrimental to the health of the individual.

Epilepsy

Epilepsy is a chronic brain condition which causes disturbances in neurons leading to repeated seizures, and can develop at any age. These seizures do not just cause a lack of consciousness, but also absences (short periods of time when someone ceases what they are doing and appears vacant or to be staring off into space; Kiriakopoulos & Obsorne Shafer, 2019), and people's awareness of what is happening around them will vary depending on the type of epilepsy they have. It has long been the case that autism and epilepsy appear to be somehow linked and that individuals who are either autistic or have epilepsy have a greater likelihood of experiencing both conditions. Even though it is not clear why there is a higher prevalence of epilepsy among the autistic population, it is thought that genetics may play a part as both conditions are highly heritable (Besag, 2017).

Autistic people with an accompanying intellectual or learning disability have a 20% chance of also having epilepsy, whereas autistic people without a learning disability have a much lower chance at 8% (NAS, 2017). In a report conducted by Autistica in 2016 on the leading causes of premature death in the autistic population, it was found that autistic people with a learning disability died on average 30 years earlier, with epilepsy being one of the main causes of this (Spiers and Autistica, 2016). It is therefore incredibly important that there is adequate support for this community. There is no evidence to suggest that epilepsy causes autism or vice versa (Besag, 2017).

Chronic Health Conditions

In a 2022 study it was found that autistic people are more likely to have a chronic health condition, classed as central sensitivity syndromes (CSS), which include conditions such as chronic fatigue syndrome (CFS)/myalgic encephalomyelitis (ME), fibromyalgia, migraine, tempo-romandibular joint disorder (TMJD), and irritable bowel syndrome (IBS), and that there is a large crossover between autistic people and those with these conditions, but it is not currently understood why (Grant et al., 2022, Grant et al., 2024). Autistic women are more prone to co-occurring physical conditions than autistic men, but it is not clear if these conditions also include those that fall under the CSS category (Grant et al., 2022, p. 2). Even though the study did not focus solely on CFS/ME, fibromyalgia, and IBS (migraine, restless leg syndrome, and TMJD were included as well), it concluded that 60% of the autistic participants met the criteria for one or more CSS (Grant et al., 2022, p. 2). It's apparent that more research is needed on the links between autism and chronic health conditions in order for people to be able to understand what is going on and how to manage their symptoms more effectively. The research made a valuable point that clinicians should not overlook the potential links between autism and chronic health conditions, even going so far as to suggest that autism screening should form part of the assessment process for CSS (Grant et al., 2022, p. 12).

Chronic Fatigue Syndrome (CFS)/
Myalgic Encephalomyelitis (ME)

CFS and ME are both conditions which have a wide range of symptoms that are experienced uniquely by each individual affected. These include extreme physical and mental tiredness that does not subside with rest, muscle pain, difficulties with concentration and memory (brain fog), sleep issues, sensory sensitivities, and gastrointestinal problems. There is currently no definitive test for CFS/ME so it is diagnosed by eliminating conditions that mimic the symptoms, including 'anaemia (lack of red blood cells), underactive thyroid gland, or liver and kidney problems' (NHS, 2024). Once these conditions have been ruled out and the symptoms are persistent for a period of more than three months, a diagnosis of CFS/ME is then considered. Even though there are crossovers between autism and CFS/ME, one key difference between them is that autism must be present from childhood, whereas CFS/ME is developed later in life, and tends to be caused by chronic stress, trauma, allergic reactions, or a virus – all of which deplete the immune system.

Fibromyalgia

People with fibromyalgia experience intense, widespread pain, along with fatigue, difficulty concentrating, gastrointestinal problems such as IBS and bloating, and problems with sleep (NHS, 2024). There are many possible triggers for fibromyalgia, including child birth, an infection, physical and mental trauma, chronic stress, or an operation (NHS, 2024). The diagnosis of fibromyalgia is conducted in a very similar way to CFS/ME with the elimination of other conditions, such as arthritis or injury. The clinician may order scans and X-rays to rule out other potential causes for the pain. If the symptoms do not go away on their own or with treatment, a diagnosis of fibromyalgia may be given.

Irritable Bowel Syndrome (IBS)/Gastrointestinal Issues

Gastrointestinal issues, such as IBS, are one of the most commonly reported medical conditions autistic people have (Madra et al., 2020, p. 1). There could be many reasons for this including restrictive eating patterns, general overall health, body mass index, anxiety, and depression.

In a 2023 study focused on autistic adults and the prevalence of gastrointestinal conditions, it was found that autistic participants with a diagnosis and those who had a higher level of autistic traits but without a diagnosis were more prone to developing gastrointestinal symptoms (Warreman et al., 2023, p. 2180). They also found that gastrointestinal symptoms were more prevalent in those who were diagnosed or scored highly on autism tests, who also had a co-occurring mental health condition such as anxiety or depression (Warreman et al., 2023, p. 2180). These findings were also mirrored in a study which indicated that autistic children with anxiety are at a higher risk of IBS due to excessive levels of cortisol in their systems (Madra et al., 2020, p. 3). Within this same study, they showed a link between pica (eating non-food items) and gastrointestinal problems, but it was unclear if pica was the cause of the gastric issues, or if people were seeking out non-food items to aid with their discomfort (Madra et al., 2020, p. 2).

Food Intolerances

Along with gastrointestinal symptoms, food intolerances are thought to be common within the autistic population. These can include gluten, lactose, and casein (protein found in dairy products), along with nuts and other foods. There is a lot of literature out there that suggests that autism is caused by food intolerances or gastro issues, which we would suggest reading with caution. Eating or cutting out certain foods will not make an autistic person suddenly not autistic, but can certainly make an autistic person a lot more comfortable and less distressed, which can only be a good thing.

Hypermobility/Ehlers-Danlos Syndrome (EDS)

There are many types of hypermobility spectrum disorders (HSD), some much more common than others. There are some overlapping traits of HSDs and autism, which include sensory differences, mental health conditions, gastrointestinal problems, and motor issues. The effect HSDs have on people range from mild to debilitating, and hypermobility is therefore thought of as a spectrum (Casanova et al., 2020, p. 2). Hypermobility of joints is fairly common, and alone is unlikely to cause serious concern or interference with daily life. Another condition that affects the joints is EDS. There are 13 types of EDS with hypermobility Ehlers-Danlos syndrome (hEDS) being the most common (Ehlers-Danlos Support UK, 2024). It is a debilitating genetic condition caused by faulty tissue throughout the body which can affect the joints, skin, and internal organs such as the bladder, stomach, and heart (Ehlers-Danlos Support UK, 2024; NHS, 2024). Other symptoms include fatigue and dizziness.

There has been research conducted on the prevalence of HSDs in the autistic population, and it has been concluded HSDs are 'over-represented' in autistic people (Glans et al., 2022).

Polycystic Ovary Syndrome (PCOS)

PCOS is caused by elevated levels of testosterone in women, which can cause cysts to form in the ovaries. The symptoms and severity differ from woman to woman but include infertility/problems conceiving naturally, heavy and/or irregular periods, hairiness, and sensitivity to sugar/carbohydrates which can lead to diabetes (NHS, 2024; World Health Organization, 2023). Research into PCOS and autism has concluded that the higher levels of prenatal testosterone in women with PCOS appears to be linked with an increased likelihood of being autistic themselves, and therefore, unsurprisingly, raises the probability of having autistic children (Cherskov et al., 2018).

Premenstrual Dysphoric Disorder (PMDD)

PMDD is a debilitating form of premenstrual tension which causes both emotional and physical side effects. These include both emotional and physical symptoms such as rapid mood changes, depression/anxiety, suicidal ideation, breast tenderness, loss of appetite, and an achy body (MIND, n.d.). This typically happens a week or two before menstruation. The exact cause of PMDD is still unknown but it appears to be genetic and may be linked to the brain responding to the changes in hormones in a more extreme way than others. It is not a hormone imbalance but instead a reaction to the changes in hormones during the luteal, or premenstrual, phase.

Even though there is little research on the topic, anecdotally, there are autistic women who suffer from PMDD. There is one study that only had 26 autistic female participants, 92% of which had experienced adverse premenstrual symptoms in line with the DSM-5 definition of PMDD (Obaydi and Puri, 2008, p. 270). As this study only used a small number of participants, it is hard to tell of the wider links between the two and it has been suggested by the International Association for Premenstrual Disorders that more research is needed in this area (IAPMD, 2024).

If PMDD is caused by how the brain reacts to the changes in hormone levels, it could be hypothesized that autistic women may be at a higher risk due to heightened sensory sensitivities to bodily changes, both emotional and physical. Further research is needed to fully understand this connection.

Other Neurodevelopmental Conditions

Even though there are similarities and crossovers between neurode-velopmental conditions, each one has its own criteria which must be individually met. They are all distinct conditions, but if you already have one neurodevelopmental condition, you have a much higher likelihood of having another. It is very difficult to find reliable sta-tistics on the percentage of people with two or more neurodevelop-mental conditions, but it is something that is widely acknowledged in both the medical field and in the wider population.

Attention Deficit Hyperactivity Disorder (ADHD) – Previously Also Known as Attention Deficit Disorder

In previous iterations of the DSM, it was stipulated that you could not be diagnosed with both autism and ADHD as it was felt that they were mutually exclusive. After much research, it was agreed upon that even though autism and ADHD appear to be the opposite of each other (autism craving familiarity; ADHD craving novelty) it is possible to have both. The previous exclusion was then taken out of the DSM-5 in 2013. More recent scientific research suggests that there could be a 50–70% co-occurrence rate of autism and ADHD. There are a number of shared features between the two, but also separate diagnostic elements as explained more fully in Chapter 6. Autistic/ ADHD people report feeling a pull between the two conditions. In summary, autism likes routines and structure and is frequently overwhelmed by daily life; ADHD likes spontaneity and variety and often seeks more stimulation than everyday life brings. The term

AuDHD has been coined to describe someone who is diagnosed or self-identifies as both, and there is a growing realization that this overlap may be more common than previously thought.

When people start taking medication to help manage their ADHD, it can 'uncover' the autism – the autism has always been there, it's just that the ADHD traits are more prominent. For instance, these people may have spent a lifetime craving routine but never been able to achieve it as the ADHD need for novelty would always win. This can also result in more heightened sensory sensitivities as well as finding socializing more tiring or anxiety inducing. Anecdotally, people feel that their ADHD 'waters down' their autism and it's only once the medication starts to work, and the ADHD is being managed, that the autism can then reveal itself in all its glory. Some people have been turned down for an autism diagnosis due to already being diagnosed with ADHD, with some doctors still assuming that you cannot have both. Another reason for being refused may be that they do not understand why you want a diagnosis of autism if you already have support/medication in place for ADHD. However, a lot of people find knowing their full neurotype to be extremely helpful as they can then utilize the right strategies and get the best support for them.

ADHD is diagnosed by a clinical psychologist or psychiatrist. The latter is necessary if medication is to be prescribed, which is the recommended first line of treatment for adult ADHD.

Dyslexia

Dyslexia is a condition which predominantly has an impact on reading and writing, due to a difficulty processing information, both written and verbal. Because of this, the effort it takes to read, write, organize tasks, and memorize information is greater than someone who is not dyslexic. Some dyslexics have visual disturbances when reading, with letters/words appearing to jump around the page, or becoming blurred. When reading it may be harder to break down new words into syllables and therefore work out what they mean or how to pronounce them. Handwriting may appear messier, and spelling not at the same level of people their own age. People with dyslexia do not have a lower than average IQ, but this may be the incorrect assumption given expectations of typical spelling and reading speed and ability in an able adult, with many adults having been told that they were 'stupid' when at school.

Dyslexia is normally diagnosed by a psychologist or specialist teacher who has specialized in specific learning difficulties. The assessor will perform a number of tests, which will include reading, analysis of handwriting style and speed, phonological awareness of real and nonsense words, memory/recall, processing speed, and visual awareness.

Dyspraxia/Developmental Coordination Disorder (DCD)

People with dyspraxia have difficulties with fine and gross motor skills, and spatial awareness. This includes writing, drawing, tying shoe laces, learning to ride a bike, playing sports, and navigating unfamiliar surroundings. It can also affect being able to tell the time, following directions/instructions, feeding oneself, and driving a car. People with dyspraxia are not just clumsy, it is more than that and for some can be quite debilitating and infuriating if the right support systems are not in place.

Dyspraxia tends to be diagnosed by an occupational therapist or an educational psychologist. They will undertake a number of tasks which will assess someone's gross and fine motor skills. To get a diagnosis of dyspraxia, your difficulties with motor skills need to be present since childhood, and cannot be explained by cerebral palsy, muscular dystrophy, or a learning disability.

As well as being a condition associated with autism due to its neurodivergent basis, dyspraxia may also be an alternative explanation for autism if some but not all autistic diagnostic elements are present; this is covered in Chapter 6, where the shared and differing features are outlined.

Sleep

Many autistic people have problems with getting to sleep, staying asleep, and feeling well rested once they wake up. The quality of sleep that autistic people get has been the subject of research, with the results undeniably reporting that autistic people tend to have a poorer quality of sleep than non-autistic people, and that this can have an impact on how they feel day to day (McLean et al., 2021). There are many different factors that can cause autistic people to struggle with their sleep pattern, including insomnia (periods of difficulties getting to sleep or staying asleep), hypersomnia (sleeping more than usual or feeling excessively tired), a lack of REM sleep (the rapid eye movement period of sleep which is the most rejuvenating), and sensory sensitivities. The majority of the research carried out on the relationship between autism and sleep is based on children, but the limited studies available on autistic adults do recognize that this is a lifelong issue for many autistic adults (Goldman et al., 2017; Schreck and Richdale, 2019). According to research, the amount of REM sleep autistic children get is less than non-autistic children – 15 vs. 25% (Buckley et al., 2010; Neumeyer et al., 2018). REM sleep is important as it helps us to process information and store memories, so if we do not have enough of this stage of sleep it can cause forgetfulness and concentration issues during the day (Summer and Summer, 2024).

Sleep disruption can also be influenced by other mental health conditions such as anxiety and depression, which are common among the autistic population. It is well known that anxiety can cause insomnia, and if someone is feeling overwhelmed by life, they may be kept up thinking about every little detail of the day and have problems switching off at night. Hypersomnia may be more common in times of autistic burnout. Burnout is commonly thought of as being a period of three or more months where someone cannot carry out their normal day-to-day activities (Raymaker et al., 2020, p. 133). Even though it is not technically classed as burnout, anecdotal evidence suggests that people can have more short-term periods of burnout that can also cause them to need to sleep more than they would normally. On the whole, autistic people have to process a vast amount of information and then mechanically work out how they respond on a daily basis. This in itself is exhausting and it is no wonder that people can feel the need to sleep more.

Sensory differences can have a big impact on how you manage to get to or stay asleep. Hypersensitivity to light, noise, smells, and touch can mean that you need your sleep environment to be just right for you. Use of blackout blinds, curtains, and eye masks, white noise machines or ear plugs, weighted blankets or certain bedding, and not sleeping next to someone can all aid with creating the right environment. Obviously everyone is different and needs different things. It is not uncommon for autistic people to travel everywhere with their own carefully chosen pillow, in order to replicate the ideal sleeping environment wherever they are.

Another factor that plays into sleep patterns for autistic people is the need for routines. Many autistic people have set wake up and going to bed times. For some, set tasks have to be carried out in the same order and way every morning and night. This brings certainty into an uncertain world. A good example of this is being away from home. The unfamiliarity this brings, not knowing what to expect or if you will be able to put your normal structures in place, can be really unsettling, and therefore disrupt your sleep pattern.

We all know that good sleep hygiene is important. If you are struggling with not being able to sleep or needing more than usual, think about ways in which you can support yourself in line with your now growing knowledge of autism and how it may relate to you.

Gender Identity and Sexuality

Although it is clearly the case that any person regardless of their sexuality or gender identity can be autistic, research has reported that there may be higher numbers of non-straight, asexual, or non-cis-gendered people in the autistic population when compared to the general population. Whilst gender and sexuality are not features of the diagnostic criteria, and nor should they be, they are worth considering in the exploration of possible autism as a means of aiding self-understanding and identifying whether they offer an alternative explanation to autism, or additional evidence pointing towards it.

With regard to sexual attraction, it has been suggested that there may be a greater number of autistic people within the asexual population (Attanasio et al., 2022), and certainly it has been our experience that some autistic people report no romantic or sexual feelings of attraction towards any person. It is also the case that autistic people experience sensory issues which may affect a willingness to engage in, and an enjoyment of, physical intimacy. They may also find the initial social interaction of meeting and ascertaining the level of interest of a new potential partner through nuanced verbal and non-verbal cues, such as flirting or subtle hints, impossible or too anxiety provoking to participate in. For others, interests and fixed schedules may take priority over sharing time and activities with a partner, both of which are generally required in a relationship.

Alexithymia and empathy may also be factors for some people regarding relationships as these can impact on the ability to identify one's own feelings and needs, and also that of others. If challenges in these areas are present, then the concept of sharing a life and feelings with another person can again feel complicated, confusing, and fraught with anxiety. This is not a matter of an autistic person being uncaring or unkind, but simply having no clue about what a partner feels or wants at any given time, and therefore no clue what to do about it. Avoidance may be the easiest path to maintain certainty and calm.

Care must be taken therefore in determining whether a person is actually asexual, or whether their autistic needs and preferences have rendered sexual activity or a relationship just too difficult or too much of an imposition to be considered worthwhile.

In one study of sexual preference, more autistic people, especially women, reported sexual attraction to partners of all genders, and more autistic women were in same-sex relationships than their non-autistic peers (Dewinter et al., 2017). In this study, a number of participants also reported 'gender non-conforming feelings' (p. 2927), and again these were reported by more autistic women (22%) than autistic men (8%).

In line with this, other recent studies suggest that there may be a higher incidence of non-cis (birth) gender and non-heterosexual identity within the autistic population, with many describing themselves as non-binary, gender-fluid, agender, or transgender. Research found that autistic children are four times as likely to report gender differences than typical children (Hisle-Gorman et al., 2019). This effect continues into adulthood where around 20% of individuals assessed in gender identity clinics present clinical level autistic features (Van Der Miesen et al., 2016). In a study examining the 'wish to be of the opposite gender' (Van Der Miesen et al., 2018, p. 2307), significantly more adolescents (6.5%) and adults (11.4%) selected this item in comparison to the general population (3–5%). Adolescent autistic birth-assigned females endorsed this more than adolescent autistic birth-assigned males, but no such gender difference was seen in autistic adults.

Anecdotally, in our experience, it is increasingly common to see non-binary, gender fluid, and trans people seeking autism assessment. Individuals describe a feeling of difference physically, mentally, and socially from their peers, not all of which they feel is adequately explained by the features of autism. For some, this early sense of not fitting in with their same-sex peers may have originated from being autistic, but possibly not knowing. There are some theories that autism itself involves a different sex hormone profile, demonstrated in the high incidence of PCOS in autistic females, which may affect gender identity, and this is commonly reported anecdotally in assessments.

Autistic people may have the experience of coming-out more than once in terms of their autistic identity and sexual and/or gender identity, and for some it can be confusing and difficult to separate one element from another. Bullying, particularly in adolescence, is common in both LGBTQIA+ and autistic populations, and it is often the case that a person feels their differences and wants to fit in, leading to masking of both autism and gender/sexuality. This may take many years to unravel and for the person's true self – in all aspects – to be identified.

Feelings of not fitting in and of being different to peers are common relating to both autism and gender, and may impact social confidence and relationships. This may be compounded by the commonly reported difficulties of relating well to same-sex peers throughout childhood and adulthood. It is very typically the case that in childhood and adolescence particularly, autistic children find their same-sex peers complicated, confusing, and not relatable. This results in them finding friendships with non-same-sex peers easier and more fulfilling, which may cause some to question their gender identity, when autism may offer a reasonable explanation for these social preferences.

However, gender identity and sexual preference generally do not affect matters of managing flexibility or sensory differences (although as mentioned above, these may hinder intimate relationships), and so despite possibly being more prevalent within the autistic population, being a person with gender difference or non-heterosexual preferences does not automatically indicate being autistic and should be addressed and supported separately.

Family History

When discovering you may be autistic, it is not uncommon to realize that pretty much everyone who is related to you also ticks quite a few of the criteria boxes. For many parents, going through the diagnostic process for a child can be the catalyst for them to seek an assessment for themselves; it might even be why you're reading this book.

Along with your own experience of these conditions, given the highly genetic nature of autism, it is also useful to take note of any family member who may be autistic or have any of the co-occurring conditions discussed in this chapter, or other health-related diagnoses. Even if those family members have not been diagnosed as autistic or ADHD, for example, but are strongly suspected to be, this can all be useful information for any formal autism diagnostic assessment, as you will typically be asked about your family history. Given the fairly recent understanding of how autism may show itself in adults, it would be reasonable to expect that many older people remain undiagnosed as autistic, and that it may be that other factors in their lives, such as alcoholism, other mental health experiences, or their unusual social or rigid habits may be all the supporting evidence that you can find.

What can be confusing is if you do not present in the exact same way as your already diagnosed/self-identified autistic family member. Just remember that all autism presents itself differently and that just because you do not have a lifelong, expert-level fascination in fishing like your Uncle Bob you cannot be autistic.

There is currently no blood or genetic test to determine whether or not someone is autistic but the consensus is that it is highly genetic. There is not one single gene that can be detected to diagnose autism, and there are likely to be many that are linked to different features of autism, but at the time of writing there is no definitive genetic evidence. But if you have a child, parent, sibling, or extended family member who has been diagnosed or suspects they are autistic, there is a much higher likelihood that you are too. Noting similarities between yourself and close relatives, especially parents, siblings, and children, can add to your background information – whether they are officially diagnosed or not.

Self-Assessment for Chapter 5 – Supporting Evidence

Consider your medical history, any previous diagnoses or ongoing health concerns as well as diagnoses and characteristics within your biological family members. The above list is not exclusive so carry out some more research on other conditions and factors that may be associated with autism and add these to the notes section at the back of the book.

Are there any other factors which may support
the idea of autism?   □ Yes □ No

Score yourself between 0 and 10 on the likelihood that you are autistic:

. . . .

Chapter 6

What Else Could It Be?

ALTERNATIVE EXPLANATIONS THAT PARTIALLY MIMIC AUTISTIC FEATURES

So, you may have gotten this far and realized that you may not be autistic after all, or at least that there is more to you than a bunch of autistic traits alone. This does not really help if you are looking for answers for why you have always felt different and not quite fitted into the world, and you may be feeling more confused than ever. Fear not!

In this chapter we will be discussing other conditions that may make you go 'aha' more enthusiastically than autism. These conditions share some features with autism and so may explain why you thought you might be autistic, but are not. Of course, you may be autistic *and* any of the following, just to make matters even more complicated. Sorry about that. Some of these are listed in the ICD-11 and we have based our list on this, as well as academic research and our experiences of assessing people. The following list contains things that may lead to a person being wrongly diagnosed as autistic, or wrongly diagnosed as any of the following instead of as autistic. If the right questions aren't asked and the responses are not taken in the correct context, missed or misdiagnosis can occur. For example, if you ask a person whether they hear voices inside their head, this may indicate psychosis or schizophrenia, or it may indicate a literal person who responds Yes because they are aware of their own thoughts chattering away inside their mind. Equally, obsessive compulsive disorder could be diagnosed if a person shares that they need to line up all of their books in a specific order and not doing so causes distress and anxiety, but this could also be an autistic feature where a person loves to keep their books in order because that is the 'right' way they should be and not doing so is irritating and wrong. The same behaviours can have different motivations and this is important. One feature does not make a diagnosis; the entire criteria must be met.

This chapter will give a brief overview of each condition, and will outline the features which are shared with autism and the differences between that condition and autism. It is once again important to remember that we are only providing information and that the detail of the condition covered is by no means exhaustive. If something feels like it fits, do your research before taking things further. To assist you to do this, we have provided sources of further information on all of the conditions mentioned in this chapter in the Resources section at the end of the book.

It is up to you to access the appropriate clinical input if you so wish – this book does not guarantee a diagnosis. You will need to make an informed decision on whether or not seeking an assessment of the following conditions is of benefit to you.

> Please note: it is not our intent that you diagnose yourself with or worry about having any serious condition. It is highly unlikely that you have a serious mental health condition which other people have not noticed. Our main purpose for including this chapter is to allow a greater understanding of conditions which are often incorrectly described and over-used in popular culture or social media and consider them in relation to autism.

Attention Deficit Hyperactivity Disorder (ADHD)

ADHD used to be thought of as a predominantly male condition, affecting children. The stereotype of a person with ADHD is someone who never sits still, talks a lot, and has very little control over themselves. They were the 'disruptive' children in the classroom. As with all neurodivergent conditions, our understanding has grown over the years and we now understand that they are more nuanced and not everyone fits the stereotype. There is now more information and understanding about how conditions like ADHD can impact people in later life and also around menopause, for example.

There are many people talking about ADHD on social media these days and it is wonderful that people with ADHD have a platform to share their experiences and are doing so, for the most part, to help others. Gilmore et al. found that the hashtag #ADHD had 6.3 billion views (2022, p. S571). However, this has led to a lot of misinformation being put out there, and many people believing that they have ADHD when they do not. This tends to be due to a handful of traits or behaviours from those who have a diagnosis, which could range from not wanting to do a boring task, to being messy, to only liking bright colours. This is something that is being seen more in clinic rooms and leading to disappointed people who have convinced themselves they have something they do not. Please do your research wisely.

There are three types of ADHD listed in the DSM-5:

- Inattentive
- Hyperactive-impulsive
- Combined – both inattentive and hyperactive-impulsive

For people over the age of 17 years seeking a diagnosis, you must meet five of the criteria – for both inattentive and/or hyperactive/impulsive features. It is also important to remember that, like autism, ADHD has to be apparent from before the age of 7 years old and has to be present in more than one setting; for example, in children this could be school and home, in adults work and home. This shows that it is not just down to a specific environment but to the individual being unable to function in a neuronormative way in all surroundings.

Here is a very brief overview of the three types and how they may impact a person in everyday life.

Inattentive Type

Someone with a diagnosis of ADHD: inattentive type will find it more difficult to concentrate on conversations and tasks, to organize their time and life responsibilities and to follow through on instructions. They will typically frequently lose things necessary for everyday life, and be easily distracted by things going on around them rather than the task in front of them. This can have an adverse effect on their ability to complete schoolwork or to engage in work, particularly if no support is given. These are the children labelled as daydreamers at school, always 'away' somewhere else in their heads. These are master procrastinators who find beginning a task almost impossible, particularly if it involves multiple steps and no quick wins of reward. ADHD: inattentive type people often struggle to find a fine line between being under- and over-stimulated, both of which can cause emotional dysregulation, poor focus and distractibility. They can find it hard to prioritize, to begin and to complete activities, often switching between tasks very quickly.

Hyperactive-Impulsive Type

This one tends to be more visibly obvious to others as it is not quite as hidden as the inattentive type, and this is particularly the case with children. For many adults their hyperactivity is internal and creates a mind that never stops whirring and thinking at great speed. People with this type have a constant need to move, talk, touch things, and make noise. They do not always think about the consequences of their actions, and may interrupt others. They may pick their fingers, bounce their leg, or be unable to sit in one position for any length of time – sometimes sitting upside down, on the floor, or in other unusual positions. ADHD: hyperactive-impulsive type people may seek risk and excitement, taking part in extreme sports, gambling or driving at speed. This is to provide the dopamine that they need and which their bodies cannot access in the same way that someone without ADHD can.

Combined Type

This a mixture of both hyperactive-impulsive and inattentive profiles as outlined above.

The consequences of ADHD for a person can be both positive and negative. These are often high-energy people with a capacity for multi-tasking, hyperfocus, and processing ideas and concepts very quickly. They can be charismatic characters with big personalities and make great leaders.

Socially, people with ADHD can find things difficult due to their tendency to be 'too much' for their peers. They may speak very quickly, loudly, and on topics which appear random and tangential to the listener. They may zone out and lose interest in conversations very quickly, interrupting and talking over others, and may also invade typical boundaries of personal space, standing very closely to someone and perhaps even touching them. There are also challenges around maintaining enough interest and motivation to finish projects that are boring or difficult, and to maintain relationships.

Dopamine is a neurotransmitter and hormone that gives feelings of reward, pleasure, and satisfaction, and there is research to suggest that some people with ADHD have lower amounts of dopamine, which is why they seek out excitement or a 'dopamine hit'. This can come in many different forms, from quick easy wins when doing daily life jobs, to liking high adrenaline situations or sport, or engaging in other dangerous behaviours and situations where the consequences were not seen or heeded. This can, in turn, cause accidents, financial problems, and in some cases problems and criminality. ADHD people can experience mental health challenges due to feelings of frustration, being out of control, and a lack of self-trust, which develops after a lifetime of making decisions which they may later consider to be ill-advised, such as driving at speed, impulsive spending, and risky behaviour, and from a constant need to change aspects of their lives which can be disruptive, such as jobs, homes, partners etc.

Shared Features with Autism

There are many Venn diagrams on the internet showing the possible similarities between autism and ADHD. These can include social and communication differences, a need for physical self-stimulation through repeated movement, sensory differences, difficulties executing plans, and intense focus on single topics.

Both can find non-verbal communication challenging in terms of reading faces and intention, and both can find reciprocal conversation, moderating voice volume and managing culturally typical personal space norms, hard to adhere to.

Both have intense topics of interest.

Both have atypical sensory profiles; although this is frequently seen, it is not mentioned in the diagnostic criteria for ADHD. ADHD individuals are often more sensory seeking than their autistic peers, who tend to be sensory avoiding. They may love bright colours in clothing and the home environment, strong tastes and smells, and a lot of visual stimulation.

Differences

ADHD is not generally accompanied by a need for routine, sameness, predictability, or certainty. There is usually no repetition of activities, meals, or schedules; in fact, this would be impossible for many ADHD people to sustain and is often entirely undesirable due to the lack of stimulation which is generated from novel experiences.

Both autistic and ADHD interests usually focus on a singular topic at one time. In autism the goal is mastery and completion, and the end of an interest, if it ever ends, is often at this point as defined by the individual. The steep learning curve is the 'hit' for autistic people as patterns, links, and concepts are connected to form understanding, and when this reaches a plateau, they may lose interest.

In ADHD, a new interest is sparked by a surge of dopamine and a 'new shiny' is found (much like a magpie seeing a reflective object). Equipment is purchased, some research is carried out, but for some, the interest wanes even before the purchases of gadgets, clothes, books, or packages of craft materials – crafts are very popular neurodivergent passions – have been opened. The books remain unread and a new favourite thing takes over, and the cycle is repeated, sometimes leading to impulsive spending and debt. In general, autistic people are far more cautious with their finances and do not impulsively spend money. The end of the interest often arrives far sooner than for an autistic person and results from the interest level dropping from 100 to 0 almost instantaneously, which may be aided by the tasks involved being 'more difficult than they looked' or boring. As a general rule, autistic people are able to stick at things and see them to completion, if interest and function is maintained, and ADHD people can find it difficult to even begin and to persevere through the tedious early stages to reach the fun stuff at the other side.

Obsessive-Compulsive Disorder (OCD)

OCD is often used flippantly to describe someone who is particularly neat and keeps all the tins in their cupboards lined up, but the reality for those who genuinely experience this condition is often much more problematic. OCD can be highly debilitating, as an individual's life is consumed by intrusive anxious thoughts and accompanying rituals. This can take up many hours of the day and involve complex avoidance strategies which can make normal life extremely difficult.

Diagnostically, a person with OCD feels compelled to perform repetitive behaviours and impulses as a response to a belief resulting from persistent and intrusive thoughts that doing so will protect them from an irrational fear that they have developed. For example, turning a light switch on and off a fixed number of times will prevent their loved ones from coming to harm. There may also be a strong need for certain thoughts or behaviours to be carried out in a prescribed sequence or number, such as counting the number of steps when climbing stairs, and for these to always be the same number. The fundamental aim of the impulses is to reduce anxiety or to gain a sense of something being complete or 'right'. Individuals with OCD typically experience no joy from these rituals and often try to resist them, but the fear and anxiety involved in not doing them is worse. There can be a sense of feeling out of control in being able to protect oneself and one's loved ones, and this may be the source of these rituals which are designed to increase a feeling of power. The person usually knows that rationally they are having no impact at all, which can increase the distress.

Shared Features with Autism

Both autistic people and those with OCD often engage in rigid, repetitive behaviours, and activities. They may place items in very precise positions and orders, finding it stressful if they are moved or disturbed.

Autistic people can find joy and comfort in repetition and can experience anxiety when things are not as expected. They may count items to ensure sameness, for example how many peas they will eat in a meal, finding that any other number is 'wrong'. They may seek repetition in clothing and foods to reduce the need for decision making and thereby reduce anxiety. The motivation for those with OCD is somewhat different: it is the desire to avoid or protect against a negative outcome, through behaviours or thoughts that are usually unrelated to the imagined outcome, or at least out of proportion or excessive as a response to it. For example, repeatedly washing hands does not prevent a person from becoming unwell when once would offer adequate protection, and checking that the front door is locked 23 times will not prevent a break-in.

Autistic people may be more likely to experience OCD due to their predisposition to anxiety and the fact they can find it cognitively difficult to deal with situations that they have no control over, such as changes, surprises, and unpredictability. All other features of the diagnostic criteria would have to be present as well as the OCD features for an autism diagnosis to be made.

Differences

OCD does not present any social or communication differences beyond those experienced by a person with severe anxiety and one who may avoid interactions and activities – and hide this avoidance – because their rituals take up a significant part of their day.

OCD does not present any intense interests unless these are connected to the fears of the individual, which become an obsessive focus and a means by which the behaviours can be justified, such as researching statistics of how many people have died eating ice cream on Tuesdays, or what bacteria is shared during a handshake.

OCD does not present any sensory differences, unless these are connected in some way to the impulses and their accompanying fears, such as only eating or avoiding certain foods, or needing to touch or be surrounded by certain objects. These decisions are not generally made due to physical discomfort created by the noise, smell, or texture of a stimuli, as is often the case in autism, but are considered to be either dangerous or protective in themselves.

Social Anxiety Disorder (SAD)

SAD (not to be confused with seasonal affective disorder) is a condition experienced by a wide range of people on either a short- or long-term basis. It may be triggered by shyness or traumatic experiences which cause a person to lose confidence in themselves around other people. Social anxiety can involve worrying intensely about forthcoming interactions and also the development of imagined scenarios where the person believes that they will be negatively perceived by others and experience embarrassment and humiliation. This can cause isolation, avoidance, and the cancellation of social situations due to this anxiety.

Shared Features with Autism

Autistic people can experience anxiety in social situations and may choose to limit or entirely avoid these events. They may believe that someone is thinking negatively about them, but due to challenges in reading non-verbal signals such as facial expressions, making eye contact, and accurately interpreting intention, they may be inaccurate.

Differences

Social anxiety disorder is not generally a lifelong condition; it can arrive and depart throughout life for those people predisposed to it, or who have had a traumatic event where they felt that others were perceiving them negatively or where they were embarrassed or ignored. Autism is lifelong.

Aside from anxiety around social interaction, those with SAD do not inherently have any social or communication differences, such as with eye contact, facial expressions, or body language. People with SAD may have typical friendships and relationships, but maintaining these in certain settings may be problematic.

SAD is not accompanied by any:

- Features requiring sameness, routines, or discomfort with change
- Sensory features which make physical environments uncomfortable
- Any intense interests

Psychosis and Schizophrenia

Schizophrenia and psychosis are mental health conditions which result in a person feeling muddled and confused due to delusions and hallucinations, which are either auditory and/or visual. The person may find it hard to distinguish between reality and their own thoughts. Psychosis is part of schizophrenia, which can additionally cause someone to withdraw from social interactions and friendships and to struggle to have the motivation to take care of themselves in terms of personal hygiene and eating properly. In the past, when knowledge of autism was more limited than it is now, there were individuals who received diagnoses of schizophrenia, which were many years later changed to autism diagnoses as this was a better explanation of their profile.

Shared Features with Autism

People who experience symptoms of schizophrenia can appear very socially withdrawn and appear to be similar to an autistic person in this regard. They may make limited eye contact and not engage in typically expected reciprocal communication comfortably. Some autistic people can find daily living and personal care difficult and can also appear to behave in ways that others may find unusual.

Differences

Psychosis and schizophrenia are rarely diagnosed prior to puberty, unlike autism which is a lifelong condition, and which can be diagnosed in early childhood (but is not always).

Psychosis and schizophrenia do not present with:

- Features of rigidity, routines and a strong preference for sameness, unless these are associated with delusions or hallucinations, or are a means by which the person can manage their daily lives
- Any intense interests
- Any sensory features beyond those experienced as a result of auditory or visual hallucinations

Borderline Personality Disorder (BPD)/ Emotionally Unstable Personality Disorder (EUPD)/Emotional Intensity Disorder (EID)

The above conditions are essentially the same but sometimes referred to by any of the above names (we shall use 'BPD' as our abbreviation for clarity and brevity).

BPD is diagnosed if a person is perceived as having difficulties in how they think about other people and themselves. The criteria are very broad which means that one person's experience of BPD may be very different to someone else's, but they are focused on emotional perceptions of relationships and oneself, which may not be accurate or helpful, and which may cause further emotional distress. Typically, someone with BPD has very intense emotions which can shift from elation to despair very quickly every few hours or few days, which can lead to them making big changes in their lives. Their sense of self can be very fragile and may change depending on who they are with at the time. This can lead to feelings of emptiness and insecurity and will usually also result in difficulties in maintaining relationships with others. Those with BPD often have a deep fear of abandonment by others with people and relationships becoming an all-encompassing focus of analysis, obsession, and frantic efforts to avoid being abandoned. Relationships are seen in a binary – perfect or terrible – way, which leads the person to sometimes act impulsively with anger or paranoia in response to these feelings. They may feel so overwhelmed by their emotions that they employ unhealthy behaviours as a means to cope with them such as substance misuse, risk-taking behaviours, self-harm, binge eating, or promiscuous sexual behaviour.

The cause of BPD is not entirely known, but is thought to be often the result of having traumatic experiences in earlier life, such as abuse, losing a parent, or instability in the home. These experiences may affect how your feelings about yourself and your relationships with other people developed in your formative years. There may also be genetic factors in the development of BPD, increasing your likelihood of having it if there are other family members who do.

There is a lot of debate about whether a BPD label is helpful or not as having a 'personality disorder' label can feel stigmatizing to some due to the lack of understanding of the condition by others. Other people find it very helpful as an explanation for how they are feeling. It is certainly the case that some people have been mistakenly diagnosed with BPD when they were in fact autistic. In our experience, this is most commonly the case in females.

Shared Features with Autism
For some autistic people, social relationships and emotions can be confusing and hard to understand, both in themselves and in other people. This can lead to hypervigilance and a tendency to analyse and become very focused on all interactions and relationships. Autistic people can develop limerence when a person becomes the focus of an intense interest, and this can lead to inaccurate beliefs about the person and the reality of the relationship that exists with them. It is also common for autistic people to experience alexithymia, which means that one's own emotions are difficult to clarify, verbalize, or express. This can lead to confusion about how one is feeling and may lead to a sense of blankness when those emotions are impossible to define. Some autistic people mask their autistic features as a means of

fitting in to achieve a sense of belonging. For some, this may include drinking alcohol or taking drugs, both to appear socially typical and to blunt some of the social and sensory discomfort of being in a social environment.

Differences

It is generally the case that BPD is not diagnosed until adolescence or adulthood, with the diagnostic criteria specifying this. Autism must be present throughout life from early childhood, but may not have a significant impact until later in life.

The rapid and extreme mood and perception changes of BPD are not a diagnostic characteristic of autism.

BPD does not present with any:

- Features of intense interests beyond that of people and relationships
- Strong need for routines, sameness, and repetition
- Sensory features

Post-Traumatic Stress Disorder (PTSD) and Complex Post-Traumatic Stress Disorder (C-PTSD)

PTSD can develop after a person has experienced or witnessed a traumatic event, with C-PTSD being when multiple traumatic events have occurred. A traumatic event is defined as one where a person has felt terrified, shocked, helpless, or horrified. There are many events that could be considered traumatic which include witnessing or experiencing death or injury – emergency medical professionals, military personnel, and victims of rape and physical attack are especially at risk. Other more mundane traumatic events may include bullying, bereavement, discrimination, and burglary.

At the time of these events, the brain is focused on survival and is in fight or flight mode, readying the body for escape or defence. Due to this focus on the immediate danger, the brain struggles to process the event as having happened in the past, and continues to relive it every time a sensory trigger such as a smell, sound, or visual object is experienced. These are called flashbacks and trigger intense anxiety and panic. Not everyone who has experienced traumatic events will develop PTSD, but there appear to be some risk factors for those who will, although these are not fully understood. The type and duration of the traumatic event(s) appear to play a part in how the trauma will be processed and women are thought to be more likely to develop PTSD than men. There are also potential differences in response depending on age, mental health, personality type, and genetic and neurobiological factors relating to the serotonin transporter gene.

Shared Features with Autism

Many autistic people have experienced multiple traumatic events throughout their lives and it may be the case that autistic people have a higher chance of developing PTSD, although the reasons for this are not clear. Autistic people tend to be hypervigilant to change and sensory triggers and can be distressed by these to the point of panic and anxiety, regardless of whether the event is considered typically traumatic or not. We know that autistic people find it difficult to tolerate and process these situations as non-threatening and their bodies enter the fight or flight state quickly. Therefore, it is entirely possible that a person may be autistic and have PTSD.

It is the case that a child with PTSD who has experienced considerable trauma in early life, in terms of abuse or bereavement, for example, may be incorrectly diagnosed as autistic as their behaviour may present as similar to that of an autistic child. They may be avoidant socially and in their communication due to fear of people, and may have difficulty managing their emotions. They may also as a result of their experiences be sensitive to loud noises or physical touch and anxious in unfamiliar situations and with change.

Differences

In general, the PTSD features which may mimic autistic characteristics are only focused on stimuli and triggers related to the traumatic events experienced rather than as a global issue for the person. For example, a person with PTSD may react very strongly to the scent of a perfume worn by their abuser, but will not have any issues with any other scents. Similarly, a person with PTSD may develop an intense interest in natural disasters, their prevalence, statistics, and likelihood of occurring, as a means of trying to protect themselves from one, but will not have shown this tendency to engage in other topics deeply for reasons of learning and joy.

In itself PTSD does not present features relating to lifelong communication, social or sensory features other than those specifically related to, and as a result of, the traumatic experience.

Traumatic Brain Injury (TBI)

TBI occurs as a result of injury to the head, most often caused by falls and road traffic accidents. There are varying degrees of TBI depending on the severity of the impact on the head ranging from dizziness to loss of consciousness. Autistic people could be at a greater risk of TBI due to head banging behaviours, coordination difficulties, or assault.

Shared Features with Autism

There may be a number of overlapping features between autism and brain injury, which would only commence after the injury has occurred rather than throughout the lifespan. Both conditions may bring challenges with communication, social relationships, and comprehension, which can lead to frustration and depression and also to a preference for repetition and familiarity. There may be sensory differences relating to pain or sensitivity to noise, smell, or taste. Both autistic people and those with TBI may find the execution of practical daily tasks difficult and may need support with these.

Differences

Autism is a lifelong condition. The features of TBI would only be noticeable after an injury has taken place. Whilst some autistic differences are likely to be shared between autism and TBI, there would typically be no intense interests.

Cultural Differences – Living in a Non-Native Culture/Language

The term 'immigrant' is not used politically or derogatively, but according to its dictionary definition as a person who lives permanently in a foreign country.

Of course, this is not a 'condition' but is a way of being which has no 'diagnosis' or 'treatment'. We thought that it was worthy of inclusion due to our experience as diagnosticians as it has come up on a few occasions where we have assessed people who are not residing in their country or culture of origin and may not be communicating routinely in their first language. Even after living in a non-native country for many years and being fluent in the language, there can be a lack of shared history, missed nuances, and shared references that can lead to feelings of difference and isolation, which can lead to thoughts about autism. The person may also be perceived as different socially and in how they live their lives by others in their adopted country, which may equally result in thoughts about why these differences may exist.

Shared Features with Autism

Immigrants and autistics can share differences such as not understanding humour, sarcasm, and other social and linguistic nuances of the adopted culture and language. Both may be considered 'rude' or direct in their communication. There may be shared discomfort in proximity of personal space, physical touch, and other sensory experiences. Both may have atypical habits and preferences and may struggle with life being unknown and unpredictable, but for different reasons.

Differences

An immigrant does not experience significant challenges when in their home country, culture, or language and it is important to investigate how the person felt and behaved in their home country and as a child. This can be more difficult if the person arrived in their foreign home during their early years. It is necessary for the person to have been perceived as atypical in their home culture, rather than only in the adopted one. Generally, there are no intense interests, repetitive behaviours, or sensory differences beyond those of familiarity, such as the consumption of specific foods or the dislike of other unknown foods. For example, if a very bland or spicy diet is the norm, then tolerating a very different taste experience may be challenging. Sensory experiences relating to personal space or physical touch will be a result of differences between the home culture and the adopted one.

Highly Sensitive Person (HSP)

The concept of the HSP was developed by psychologists Elaine and Arthur Aron, and featured in Elaine Aron's book *The Highly Sensitive Person* (1996) and describes a personality trait also called sensory processing sensitivity (SPS) – this is not the same as sensory processing disorder (SPD), which we will discuss later in this chapter. SPS brings a deeper awareness of sensory stimuli, whereas SPD involves a challenge for the brain in processing and organizing sensory stimuli (light, sound, smells etc.). SPS has been academically studied and is considered to be experienced by 10–20% of the population, and is seen across cultures and in many animal species as a typical biologically based temperament trait. Links have been made between HSP and autism, with some believing that HSP is simply a subset of autistic features and that all HSP are autistic, and others who see overlaps and differences between the two. In recent years, the HSP has become a popular idea in self-development and a number of people seeking autism assessment describe themselves as such. It is often the case that these individuals had assessed themselves to be a HSP, but then had read about the link between HSPs and autism, and identified additional characteristics in themselves which were beyond those of the HSP profile, which led them to consider the accuracy and completeness of their assessed HSP profile. There can be some reluctance to recognize that one may be autistic rather than a HSP as there is generally more stigma related to an autism diagnosis.

Features of HSP/SPS relate to a disposition which is sensitive to sensory inputs such as noise, smells, lights, and busy places. An individual with HSP/SPS will become easily over-stimulated in such environments. They may be highly sensitive to caffeine, pain, and hunger, but also have an ability to notice and enjoy fine food, delicate smells, and beautiful environments. The trait also affects mental and emotional experiences with the person being easily distressed by upsetting events, movies, and people. They may seek to withdraw from daily activities to find calm and have a deep inner world. Typically called shy or sensitive as a child, these individuals can experience high levels of stress and SPS has been linked to anxiety, agoraphobia, ADHD, and trauma.

Shared Features with Autism

Both HSPs and autistic people can find sensory stimulating environments overwhelming and may require recovery time and strategies to avoid and manage these, such as noise-cancelling headphones and time alone. Both groups can find social situations difficult when there are large groups of people, but for different reasons. Both HSPs and autistic people can have a rich inner world where they retreat to escape, but this is not the case for all autistic people, some of whom have few internal thoughts.

Differences

Whilst sensory experience is a key feature of both HSP and autism, and in both it can be heightened, this is not always the case for autistics who can be both hypo- and hypersensitive to various stimuli. Some autistic people love loud noises, strong smells and tastes, and firm physical touch. HSPs can focus deeply on a sensory experience – particularly the emotional elements of it – where autistic people can often be overwhelmed by the sheer range of stimuli that is bombarding them. The HSP can usually recover quickly with withdrawal and rest.

Autistic people enjoy repetition, familiarity, and intense interests in singular topics. These are not simply activities which avoid stress and allow calm – as in the case of the HSP – but which are actively and positively sought. HSPs do not seek the level of routine, sameness, and predictability that an autistic person typically does, and this would only be necessary as a means of managing sensitivity – for example, only travelling by public transport at certain times of the day when it is quieter. In contrast, an autistic person may choose to do so to ensure that all elements of the journey are repeatable due to challenges in the contextual thinking required to generate alternative plans and tolerate changes to expectations.

Whilst not the case for all autistic people, some find understanding and experiencing emotions and having typical empathic responses to others challenging. The core of being a HSP is to have a deep sensitivity to one's own feelings and those of others.

In general, a HSP does not present lifelong differences in communication, social interaction, or relationships beyond what is affected by their high sensitivity to over-stimulating people or environments. In fact, HSPs are considered to have highly attuned people skills, which does not reflect the diagnostic criteria for autism.

Attachment Disorder

A diagnosis of attachment disorder is generally only given in childhood although adults can continue to experience the impact of its features. Either way, it is a condition which originates in childhood and is seen in those who have had severe disruption to their relationships with parents and/or carers in the form of absence through illness or abandonment, abuse or neglect, whether physical or emotional. Attachment disorder is a likely outcome for those who had multiple changes of primary caregiver, in the case of those who spent time in care with multiple foster carers or homes, or with various different family members. The absence of typical relationship development at this early stage can affect how individuals with attachment disorder communicate and interact with others throughout life. It is often the case that they did not have the role models or opportunities to learn the give and take of social relationships in the same way that their peers did or that their relationships were harmful and abusive in some way leading to the learning of unhealthy relationship rules. Attachment disorder can also cause fear and anxiety in new and unfamiliar situations resulting from the child experiencing a lot of unpredictability and upheaval due to their unstable or difficult home environment. This can lead to those affected being inflexible and fixed in their daily activities as they seek a sense of security in the known. There may also be sensory issues, which may relate to noise and touch as a result of traumatic experiences.

In adults, there may be difficulties in establishing and maintaining healthy relationships, finding social situations stressful, and experiencing anxiety and depression. It is important to note that for attachment disorder to be considered as a possible explanation for challenges in adulthood, there must have been very significant disruption to early childhood relationships with primary caregivers.

Shared Features with Autism

The communication and social profiles of autistic people and those with attachment disorder can appear very similar in childhood, but may have different root causes. Eye contact may be avoided and solitude sought. Both may share challenges in reciprocal conversations, chat, and developing friendships and relationships. For autistic people, there may be lifelong neurodevelopmental differences in observing, processing, and responding to social and linguistic cues that lead to awkwardness and a desire to spend time alone. For those with attachment disorder, the absence of communication and interaction when young may lead to a lack of skill and practice in these areas, and a lack of understanding of why they may have value, and so they may be actively avoidant of any physical affection or social interaction.

Both may require routine and rigid structures, with autistic people finding it necessary for life to be manageable due to a difficulty in thinking flexibly about change, and those with attachment disorder seeking stability as a result of early experiences of disruption.

A child with attachment disorder may develop an obsession with food because they were often hungry and learned to steal, hide, and hoard it, whereas an autistic child is more concerned about the texture, presentation, and other qualities of the food they are given. Other sensory features may appear in both conditions, but in attachment disorder these are more likely to be focused around responses to previously experienced traumatic events, such as issues with affection and physical touch arising from abuse.

Differences

Autistic people are usually quite straightforward and without agenda in their communication, often being very truthful or struggling to tell lies convincingly due to difficulties mentalizing (imagining what someone else may be thinking or is likely to believe to be true). Those with attachment disorder are often able to lie well in order to make themselves appear more successful in some way than they are or to deflect blame away from themselves. They are often hypervigilant to the moods and feelings of others due to their past experiences and able to react to these quickly and in an over-responsive way to ensure their own safety, which they have learned is necessary.

Autistic people are concerned with fairness and rules, especially in play and activities. Those with attachment disorder are happy to break rules and have a greater focus on winning than fairness, having not experienced or been taught the value of sharing and considering others.

Dyspraxia/Developmental Coordination Disorder (DCD)

Dyspraxia is a condition of movement and coordination. In children, early physical milestones that require either gross or fine motor skills are typically delayed. These include actions such as crawling and walking, feeding oneself, and dressing (tying shoe laces, using zippers, buttons etc.). In adults, these challenges continue with a general clumsiness in all areas of life. Dyspraxics may find that they have never mastered the art of riding a bicycle, dancing in time, or catching a ball. Changing direction when walking, balance, and tripping up stairs are further examples of gross (large movement) motor skills. With fine movements, mess is often the result for a dyspraxic person: shaving, applying make-up, cooking, and using cutlery can all be effortful and problematic. Alongside these physical differences, dyspraxia can also bring related features in other areas. Speech may be fast and loud, with words out of sequence and unclear. There may be sensory differences, poor senses of direction and difficulties estimating time, speed, and distance. Dyspraxia also affects concentration, processing of information, handwriting, memory, and the ability to plan and organize. In summary, an adult dyspraxic may appear scattered in their words, thoughts, and daily functioning, unkempt and physically awkward.

Shared Features with Autism

Both autism and dyspraxia can present as both physical and social awkwardness, clumsiness and delayed developmental milestones in childhood. In adulthood, both can appear somewhat eccentric in their speech and shared thoughts and find the organization and execution of daily living tasks, such as personal care, meal planning, household chores, and finances difficult.

Differences

Dyspraxia does not present with any features around rigidity, sameness, and repetition. There is no requirement for a fixed schedule of routines, ordering of tasks or categorizing of objects. The only challenges with changes relate to the effort involved for the person in mentally and physically coordinating themselves for the new situation. For example, if someone is required to move to a different seat in a room, this requires considerable bandwidth to carry out the task without bumping into something or someone, breaking or spilling something, or injuring oneself.

Dyspraxia does not generally present with the same level of sensory differences as autism. There may be tactile defensiveness – a dislike or sensitivity to touch – but generally dyspraxic individuals are not as impacted by sensory stimuli as autistic people can be.

There are no intense interests specially indicated in the dyspraxia profile.

Social Communication Disorder (SCD)

SCD is a recently established diagnosis mentioned for the first time within the DSM-5 which essentially mirrors the communication and social diagnostic criteria for autism only, with no other features present.

Shared Features with Autism

As is the case for autistic people, those with SCD find communication, whether verbal or non-verbal, challenging within a neurotypical environment. Sarcasm, jokes, and hidden agendas may be difficult to comprehend and facial expressions hard to read, detect meaning from, and respond to. The criteria for both conditions include differences in the desire and involvement in sharing emotions and experiences, the reciprocal back and forth of conversations, and adjusting language to different contexts, such as recognizing social hierarchies or the age and comprehension level of the audience.

Differences

SCD does not identify any features relating to routines, sameness, intense interests, or sensory differences.

Sensory Integration Disorder (SID)/ Sensory Processing Disorder (SPD)

Although not recognized as a distinct medical condition, SID/SPD is sometimes a term used in diagnosis – especially of children – and so we include it here because the concept may be useful, even if the term is not recommended for diagnostic usage. There are sensory messages being received both externally and internally at all times and the organization, analysis, interpretation, and modulation of these allow us to get our needs met and to continually restore levels of comfort. Sounds, lights, smells, pain, temperature, balance, taste, and touch all provide us with information. These sensory inputs are received by our eyes, ears, skin, joints, internal organs, and brains. For example, feelings of hunger alert us to find food, sensations of itchiness lead us to cut out the offending label or have a scratch. If we hurt ourselves, we might instinctively cry out or shout for help, which will bring someone to our aid. For the most part we respond to these sensory stimuli quickly and intuitively, with most of the signals we receive not causing any issue, attention, or distress. We don't even notice most of the sounds, smells, and sensations that we are bombarded with on a constant basis.

This is not the case for someone with SPD, for they experience one or more sensory stimuli in a more extreme way – either with more sensitivity than is typical ('hyper'), or less ('hypo'). Each individual person may have a mixture of a hyper and hypo sensory profile, with some information being received with great intensity, such as sound, and others, such as pain, not received very much at all. A person with hypersensitivity to a sensory input will perceive even a small amount of this stimuli as very overwhelming, when the majority of people would not find this to be the case at this level. If this person is hypersensitive to smell, they may not be able to use any toiletries that have any perfume at all, and those who share their household may also be required not to do so. They may be highly sensitive to odours and be able to smell every single ingredient in a dish. In contrast, someone with hypersensitivity to smell may seek and use very strong fragrances because they need them to be very concentrated in order for them to be detected. This person may not smell when food is off, or when there is a gas leak or a fire.

SPD can affect the ability to manage a range of daily activities such as hair or teeth brushing, eating a wide range of foods due to taste, smell, and/or texture, having sticky hands, showering, crossing roads safely, fireworks, wearing certain clothes and shoes, tolerating bright lights, background noise, and ticking clocks. It can also bring enormous pleasure to those whose sensitivity can allow them to experience music, physical touch, or taste to a level that most people could never access. However, the negative outcomes of living with SPD can be both physical in terms of discomfort, and mental as a result of feeling assaulted and therefore exhausted by the sensory elements of everyday life.

Shared Features with Autism

SPD and autism both share atypical perceptions of the whole range of sensory experiences, both hyper and hypo, both seeking and avoiding, both unpleasant and joyful. The sensory profile of an individual in both SPD and autism may be typical in some senses, hypo in some and hyper in others. Both may engage in behaviours to either seek or avoid these stimuli, depending on how they are perceived. These behaviours may appear repetitive and obsessive.

Differences

SPD does not present any differences in communication or social interaction, unless these are as a direct result of either seeking or avoiding sensory stimuli, such as not being able to attend school or social events purely due to the noise, lights, or proximity of other people, and not due to the interactions themselves.

SPD does not present any features of repetition or inflexibility, unless these are as a direct result of the sensory impact of the choice. For example, a person with SPD may only wear a limited range of clothing, or eat a restricted range of food solely to meet their sensory needs, rather than having a preference for sameness, repetition, or familiarity in and of itself.

SPD does not present any intense interests, again unless these are directly related to managing the sensory environment. For example, someone with SPD may become an expert in perfumes due to their highly sensitive sense of smell, which brings them enormous pleasure, rather than discomfort.

Giftedness

There is no official or agreed definition of giftedness, nor is it a 'condition'; rather it is an advanced ability in one or more subjects or areas of learning when compared with peers of the same age, environment, and experience. Gifted individuals are able to learn, think, analyse, memorize, and recall information at a high level. They are often very insightful and considered intense and serious as children. In IQ tests, a gifted person will score above 130 (with the average person scoring around 100), with profoundly gifted people scoring over 160.

Despite the great benefits of having the ability to think and process information at a high level quickly and easily, some gifted people struggle to reach their potential. There can be social challenges both in childhood and adulthood if the person cannot find peers who are at the same intellectual level or who do not share the same interests leading to loneliness. Many gifted people learn early on in their lives that being the smart one can lead to them being bullied, teased, and excluded, and so they deliberately mask their abilities, for example by electing not to answer questions in class, to avoid standing out. In adult life, if fulfilling employment cannot be found, a gifted person can drift from job to job becoming increasingly frustrated and depressed.

Shared Features with Autism

Not all gifted people are autistic, although this is often assumed to be the case and there are clearly a number of people who are both. The overlap of giftedness and autism (or other neurodevelopmental conditions) is described as 'twice exceptionality' – often abbreviated as '2e'. These individuals are noted as having high intellectual ability alongside significant challenges. Whilst there is no mention of IQ or ability within the diagnostic criteria for autism, the 'savant' profile of an individual with one or more extraordinary skills accompanied by severe challenges in daily living, for example, was the popular view of autistic people for a long time, such as in the movie *Rain Man*.

Common traits between autism and giftedness include social difficulties, which may stem from thinking at a different speed and complexity to one's peers in the case of giftedness, or from a different way of processing social cues as is the case in autism. Both may have intense, singular interests which are all-encompassing and engaged in to a great depth, acquiring extensive knowledge and skill. Both may also share some challenges with daily living and organization, finding the mundane and abstract more difficult to manage than the complex and linear.

Differences

Giftedness alone does not necessarily present social or communication challenges and individuals may have a typical understanding of social and linguistic norms and establish and maintain typical relationships throughout their lives. They may enjoy social events and have no strong need for advance warning of changes, routines, or sameness. Their thinking may be very flexible and able to adapt to new and changing information and concepts, which an autistic person can find hard to do as they may tend to have a more binary (black-and-white), all-or-nothing thinking style. Giftedness alone does not generally present with sensory differences or challenges with multi-tasking.

Self-Assessment for Chapter 6 – Alternative Explanations

Remember that it is possible to have autism as well as another condition, but that all of the diagnostic features of autism must still be met. Look at your notes from Chapter 1 and see if there are any gaps in how you meet the criteria. Is there a condition from the list above that better fits your profile of abilities and experiences? The list in the chapter is not exhaustive, so further research may also help to answer this question, if your notes from the chapter are not definitively in favour of you meeting all of the diagnostic criteria.

Is autism still the best explanation for your
experiences? ☐ Yes ☐ No

Score yourself between 0 and 10 on the likelihood that you are autistic:

. . . .

Chapter 7

Screening Tests

FIRST STEPS TO FINDING OUT

It may be that your path towards suspicions of autism began by completing an online autism screening test via social media or elsewhere online. The AQ-50 (Autism Quotient 50) has perhaps been the most widely shared across the years and pops up on Facebook and Reddit feeds from time to time. You may have completed it, or any other autism test, with mild curiosity and been surprised or reassured by your score. There are several autism tests and quizzes online with variable reliability and academic stringency. Some are excellent and others contain items or questions which, although they may be anecdotally common experiences for autistic people, do not meet any of the clinical diagnostic criteria, and hence do not provide any evidence for a formal diagnosis. Whilst it can be personally helpful to know that many other people share your experiences, it can lead to a false belief that you are autistic, and hence a surprising assessment outcome. Care should be taken then to where supporting evidence is gathered from.

The following screening tests have all been developed from a stringent academic base. Their reliability across different groups – age, gender, intellectual capacity – may vary, but comparing scores from several screening tests should give you at least an indication of the presence of some diagnosable autistic features. It should be noted, however, that these are only screening tests to determine the value and likely outcome of an autism assessment, and are not a diagnosis in themselves, because they do not include all aspects of the diagnostic criteria and do not clarify the reasons why a person has responded to a question or statement in the way that they did. There are other reasons why a person may score within the autistic range in a screening test and not be autistic. For example, in our experience, people with extremely high intellectual ability can feel that they struggle socially with (less intellectually able) peers and are highly logical, and yet they do not meet the full criteria for autism. Similarly, some people are highly anxious – both socially and otherwise – and this can lead them to avoid social situations and to manage their life very rigidly to manage change, but again do not meet the criteria for diagnosis. As mentioned previously, it is the 'why' you do or don't do something rather than the behaviour itself that determines autism's presence.

It is also the case that some people will score in the range expected by a non-autistic person but in fact be autistic. This may be because they are not very self-reflective or aware of their differences – someone else scoring the test on their behalf may answer the same questions very differently. For example, this person may feel that they are very flexible and highly social, but their perspective may not be based on an accurate assessment of how most people live their lives. This is not to say that they are wrong per se, only that the nature of the screening tests is to identify differences from typical behaviour, and they assume that you know what this is. Another reason for a less than clear outcome or a lower than expected score from the tests is where there are comorbidities: two or more neurodiverse conditions such as autism and ADHD together. This mixed profile can alter the experience of each condition, and whilst both sets of diagnostic criteria must be met, sometimes certain facets of one condition can be diluted a little by the compensatory features of the other. For example, where an autistic person may be seen to be rigid around their routines, a person with comorbid ADHD may require novelty and task shifting to maintain attention and may appear as more spontaneous, even though this may not be the case.

All of the following tests contain a series of statements or questions and you are required to decide whether you agree or disagree with how true each of them are for you. Some of the statements may make you think 'it depends on the situation', so it is helpful to consider what is generally true when you do not have any coping mechanisms in place. For example, if you are comfortable in social situations only when with familiar people or when using alcohol, and otherwise may experience anxiety or not attend, then it would be reasonable to say that you are not comfortable in social situations. These tests – and the diagnostic process itself – are looking for differences when compared with a typical person. For example, a typical person would not usually experience discomfort being around people most of the time and not require alcohol to facilitate their attendance. They would also generally not require a lot of information in advance of a social event, or for arrangements to be adhered to precisely in terms of timings, sequence, who will be there, and destination.

The test statements can also be difficult to respond to if you do not know very many typical people, because like many autistic people, you may have surrounded yourself by other neurodiverse or otherwise similar people, or don't have much sense about whether your behaviour is atypical or not – remember, there is no judgement being made here about your behaviour, only an assessment of its diversion from how most people think and behave. If you don't spend much time with other people or have any clue about what they do and why, it can be difficult to make this judgement.

It can be helpful to ask people who know you well to also complete these tests on your behalf in order to get a broader view of your profile. Make sure that the people that you ask truly see who you are, otherwise you may experience more self-doubt if their responses indicate a very different view than you yourself have. If those close to you are autistic, they may not consider you to have any atypical behaviour at all, because it is just the same as their own.

The scoring ranges for these tests between typical and autistic behaviour are quite wide and so a single statement answered 'wrongly' will generally not make a great deal of difference to the overall outcome. For example, the mean typical score for the AQ 50 test is around 16 out of 50 statements and the mean autistic score is 35, which is a large number of the statements answered with the completely opposite response. The idea with the screening tests is not to be too concerned with specific scores, but to get a sense of whether you typically score within or outside of the ranges expected for autistic people. If you are consistently scoring in an inconclusive mid-range on a number of the screening tests, then this may indicate autism, particularly if you found the questions confusing and difficult to answer. It may also indicate no autism but something else which warrants further investigation, such as social anxiety, OCD, or ADHD. In this case, it may be worth looking deeper into your test scores to see if there is a pattern of statements that you consistently score in an autistic/non-autistic way, which may give clues as to whether aspects of socializing, rigidity, interests, masking, or communication are your areas of strength or challenge. All of these need to be present for an autism diagnosis, so any 'gaps' may provide insight into what is going on. If you consistently score well outside of the ranges expected for an autistic person, it is highly likely that you are not autistic, or you have not understood the questions at all. Scores across several tests which are all within the expected ranges for an autistic person would suggest a high likelihood that you are autistic, and this would warrant further investigation.

All of these screening tests are available online and, with the exception of the SAAT, all are available and beautifully and fully explained on the Embrace Autism website listed in the Resources section, which is a fantastic resource written by a team of autistic people.

Some of the tests have been translated into several languages for the ease of people whose first language is not English, and you may be able to find these online. We present here a brief overview of each test and its scoring thresholds and recommend that you complete several different ones and compare your results. You should see a pattern emerging of any autistic tendency.

Links to websites which have online versions of all of the tests below (except the SAAT, which at the time of writing was not yet available) are provided in the Resources section at the end of the book. Scoring ranges and a space for your test scores can be found at the end of this chapter.

Self-Assessment of Autistic Traits (SAAT)

The recently developed SAAT test is unique in its design and development in that it is a self-assessment measure of autistic traits as described by the lived experience of autistic people, rather than those observed by non-autistic researchers and clinicians. It is also designed for autistic adults with higher verbal and intellectual ability and suitable for those who have learned to mask or compensate for their autistic features. The test does not appear to be available online at the time of writing (July 2024), but this may change in the future. You can read about the development and ethos of the test in the paper 'Centering the inner experience of autism: Development of the self-assessment of autistic traits' (Ratto et al., 2023).

Autism Quotient (AQ-50 and AQ-10)

The AQ-50 and AQ-10 (shortened version used by GPs to quickly assess whether a person may benefit from a referral for diagnosis) consists of a number of statements – either 50 or 10 – to which you must agree or disagree to achieve a score. Despite being given the options to 'slightly agree' or 'slightly disagree', the scoring does not reflect this and you actually just have 'agree' or 'disagree' choices. The AQ was developed in 2001 and some regard it as somewhat outdated in the wording of some of its questions as understanding of autism has changed since then. However, its validity remains high and it is a good indicator of likely autistic features.

A score of 26 or above out of 50 indicates a likelihood that you are autistic and 79.3% of autistic people score 32 or higher.

The Camouflaging Autistic Traits Questionnaire (CAT-Q)

The CAT-Q does not test for all of the diagnostic criteria for autism but focuses on the amount that a person masks or hides their autistic characteristics. These are subdivided into three categories:

- Compensation – conscious learning and adopting of strategies and mimicking behaviour to manage social situations
- Masking – deliberately hiding autistic characteristics to appear 'normal' or invisible
- Assimilation – adapting behaviour to fit in with those around you

The test consists of 25 statements to which you have 7 options of agreement/disagreement. It has good validity and is a helpful addition to the list of screening tests as it looks at a more recently identified tendency in autism, particularly females, of masking behaviours which may hide typical autistic presentation and make diagnosis more difficult. The scores range from 25 to 175 and the autistic threshold is a score of above 100.

The Ritvo Autism Asperger Diagnostic Scale – Revised (RAADS-R)

The RAADS-R is an 80 statement test which asks you to respond whether the statement is true now, when younger, or not true. It covers the entire diagnostic criteria in subsections for language, social relatedness, sensory-motor and circumscribed interests. The RAADS-R test is considered to have very good reliability and accurately identifies autistic features. Some criticisms of the test are related to the language used which appears outdated and makes assumptions about what constitutes 'normal' behaviour and what is a 'close friend', for example. Some autistic people find these questions difficult to answer as they have no means of comparison between themselves and whatever 'normal' is.

The maximum possible score is 240 and the threshold for possible autism is 65, but this score needs to cover all of the four subscales to a prescribed threshold in each one. The mean score for autistic people is 130.

The Aspie Quiz

The Aspie Quiz has 119 questions and measures the following across five domains: talent, perception, communication, relationship, and social. The scores range from 0 to 200, with 140 or above suggesting that you are 100% likely to be 'atypical'. The quiz tests for autism and neurotypicality, giving a percentage likelihood for each. Some items do not appear to specifically relate to the diagnostic criteria and as a result you may not meet the threshold on this test when you do on others. It does, however, produce an interesting diagram which maps your profile and may also indicate other neurodiversities.

Systemizing Quotient – Revised (SQ-R)

The SQ can accompany the AQ to assess the tendency to make sense of the world in a systematic way, that is to use logic, analysis, and pattern recognition. This is not a test of all of the features of autism, but is a useful addition to building your level of certainty about whether you may be autistic, particularly if you have a strong leaning towards a preference or need for structure, rules, and categorizing.

The test has 75 items which are agreed/disagreed with leading to a possible maxim score of 150. A score of 75 or above indicates autistic features, and the average score is 77.2 for autistic people and 55.6 for neurotypical people.

Empathy Quotient (EQ)

The EQ can be used to accompany the AQ to assess the ability to understand the perspectives of others. There is much debate in the autistic community about the concept of empathy and the long-held suggestion that autistic people do not feel empathy. This leads to the implication that autistic people are not capable of caring about and for others which is entirely untrue. What this test appears to show is that autistic people can have differences in how they perceive social interactions and communication, and it does so with good validity.

The test consists of 60 statements, 20 of which are filler questions, which are not scored. A score of 30 or below indicates autistic features and 81% of autistic people are below this score. It is important to note that achieving a very low score does not mean that you are a psychopath or a danger to people; it is more likely an indication of a difficulty in reading verbal and non-verbal social cues and of intuitively knowing social rules.

Repetitive Behaviours Questionnaire (RBQ-2A)

The more recently (2015) developed RBQ-2A focuses on the tendency towards sameness and routines in terms of activities, and also repetitive motor behaviours, such as rocking or flapping. The test only covers this one element of the diagnostic criteria and does not examine social or communication experiences.

There are 20 questions which ask you to report the frequency that you engage in certain behaviours. Scores range between 20 and 60, with the possible autistic threshold being over 26. The typical autistic score is 36. The RBQ-2A is good at identifying potentially autistic behaviours, but someone who experiences OCD or movement conditions such as Tourette syndrome may also score highly and not be autistic. The results of this test need to be considered alongside other screening tests.

Self-Assessment for Chapter 7 – Screening Tests

By now, you have probably taken all of the above tests several times and hopefully come to some conclusions about your possible autisticness and/or other explanations for why you decided to read this book. Given all that you have read so far, you may have some thoughts about whether it's time to confidentially self-diagnose or consider a diagnostic assessment of some sort.

Test Name	Typical Autistic Scoring Range	Your Score
AQ50	26–50	
AQ10	6–10	
CAT-Q	100–175	
RAADS-R	65–240	
The Aspie Quiz	140–200	
SQ	75–150	
EQ	0–30	
RBQ-2A	26–60	

Score yourself between 0 and 10 on the likelihood that you are autistic:

. . . .

Chapter 8

Decision Time

TO BE OR NOT TO BE AUTISTIC

You've read the criteria, completed all of the screening tests, and ruled in or out a whole variety of other possibilities. Now, it is time to collate all of your scores and thoughts and consider whether you have enough evidence to feel confident that either self-diagnosing as autistic or seeking assessment may be a helpful next step, or whether answers in a different direction make more sense.

Circle Yes or No to indicate whether you feel you meet each required element of the diagnostic criteria and for all of the following chapter summaries.

Chapter 1 – Meeting the Diagnostic Criteria

Communication and language	☐ Yes	☐ No
Social relationships	☐ Yes	☐ No
Flexibility of thought/executive functioning	☐ Yes	☐ No
Sensory differences	☐ Yes	☐ No
Intense interests	☐ Yes	☐ No
Repetitive movements	☐ Yes	☐ No
Above features seen across lifespan – childhood and adulthood	☐ Yes	☐ No

Chapter 3 – Reasons for Considering Autism

Does your reason for suspecting autism resonate
with others?   ☐ Yes ☐ No

Chapter 4 – Reasons Why I Can't Be Autistic

Have your reasons why you can't be autistic
been explained?   ☐ Yes ☐ No

Chapter 5 – Supporting Evidence

Are there any factors which may support the
idea of autism?   ☐ Yes ☐ No

Chapter 6 – Alternative Explanations

Is autism still the best explanation for your
experiences?   ☐ Yes ☐ No

Chapter 7 – Screening Tests

Are your scores consistently within the
expected autistic range?   ☐ Yes ☐ No

I am sure that you have worked out by now that the more Yeses you have circled, the more likely it is that an autism assessment or self-diagnosis would make sense for you. If you have concluded that you are unlikely to be autistic, proceed to Chapter 10. Alternatively, if your outcome suggests that self-diagnosis or formal assessment may have value, then move on to Chapter 9.

Chapter 9

Self-Diagnosis and Diagnostic Assessment

Approaching your GP for an autism diagnosis may fill you with dread. Having to sit in a doctor's office and fear being dismissed or not believed is never going to be a nice experience. So we are here to help you get the best out of the appointment. First, you may be feeling that you are wasting your GP or other medical practitioner's time by even asking for a diagnosis. You may feel that you are being foolish seeking an assessment at your age and that perhaps it is unnecessary, especially if you have managed to look after yourself so far in life on your own. We would urge you to try and overcome these doubts and worries. The value of a confirmation that you are autistic (or not), can be life changing for many people as it tells them who they really are and allows them to get support at work, home, or in education, but mostly in their own minds. This knowledge can decrease or even eradicate decades of mental health issues simply by having a better understanding of the root cause of the anxiety or depression, and can certainly provide guidance to finding more appropriate tools to treat these conditions, when perhaps standard therapy, for example, hasn't been successful. There is no reason to deny yourself access to this process and possibly the 'relief' that so many people describe when discovering that they are autistic. If it turns out that you aren't autistic after all, that's OK too, and you won't have been wasting anyone's time. You simply eliminated a possibility. You can't be expected to be an expert in diagnosis, which is why you go to a professional person in the first place. Please go and get the help you need. Remember, we told you earlier that the oldest person we have assessed was 87 years old and it was a valuable and emotional experience for her.

So, how to proceed with speaking to a medical practitioner about your potential autism?

First, perhaps take some notes about how you want to broach the topic. They may ask why you think you're autistic, so you may want to share how you came across the idea: your therapist suggested it, a family member has been diagnosed etc. You may take some sample tests with you to share your scores. Above all, gather and take:

Evidence, evidence, evidence.

The more you have that backs up your suspicion of autism, the harder it will be for the doctor to ignore or dismiss you, which sadly has often been the case for many adults that we have assessed. There may be a referral process carried out by a GP before you can access the actual assessment itself, so it is necessary to provide enough information to get through this first step. Be prepared for them to ask why an autism diagnosis is so important to you, as you have reached adulthood without needing one, so think about your response to this question in advance. Once you have been referred for a diagnosis and are waiting to be assessed, it will again be beneficial to provide evidence of pre-existing mental health, physical, or neurodivergent conditions such as dyspraxia, anxiety, or hypermobility. Any reports you may have can be very helpful to provide your diagnostician with, as this information can aid in your diagnosis process. Most diagnosticians understand that there is a higher likelihood that you may be autistic if you have any of the supporting evidence listed in the earlier chapters. There is space to list these in the Notes section in the Appendix.

Self-Diagnosis – Pros and Cons

The concept of self-diagnosis, usually reserved for independent and intellectually able adults who can do their own research and come to their own conclusions, is where a person decides that they believe themselves to be autistic and do not undertake any form of external assessment.

Within the neurodiversity community, there are individuals who feel strongly about self-diagnosis and who are resistant to the idea that a medical professional is the only person who can determine whether a person is autistic or not and seek to claim this identity for themselves on their own terms. For other people, formal assessment or diagnosis is not an option due to location, cost, availability of suitable services, or other reasons. In countries where state healthcare provides free assessments, wait times can be several years in length and referral processes hard to navigate – sometimes the gatekeepers of the referral are not educated or knowledgeable about adult autism. The quality of the assessment service can be variable, particularly if you are female, or have any other atypical profile or accompanying disability or condition. For many people, paying for a private assessment would be their only option, but the cost of this can be prohibitive. There is also the issue of trusting the medical process and feeling confident that the diagnostician will get it right. This is particularly the case if you have had several negative experiences with medical professionals and have not felt heard or understood. In the case of state-funded assessments, there is not likely to be any choice in who carries out the assessment (except currently the England's Right to Choose scheme) and what diagnostic procedures are used. Only those who can afford to pay will have some access to that luxury.

The process of arriving at a confident self-diagnosis of autism can be a tricky one. Many people do their research and find information online, but care must be taken over the accuracy and quality of this as there is a lot of misinformation on social media and other websites, which can lead to incorrect and inaccurate understanding of what is actually autism and what is not. Some people struggle with a continuing sense of self-doubt about their self-diagnosis for some time, leading them to become obsessed with trying to determine categorically that they are autistic through extensive research and taking numerous online screening tests (Lewis, 2016). Over time, for many people their certainty and confidence can grow to the point where they are satisfied with their conclusion and comfortable in accessing the autistic community, disclosing to those close to them and fully accepting and embracing their autistic identity.

For others, self-diagnosis is a temporary measure whilst waiting for a formal assessment. One study found that people waited on average 3.25 years before receiving a formal diagnosis (Lewis, 2016), for the reasons stated above and others. If a formal assessment is undertaken at a later date, it may be disappointing if the outcome does not agree with your self-diagnosis and provide the validation and confirmation of long-held beliefs about being autistic, especially if you have been 'out' as an autistic person prior to the assessment. In this situation, it may be that you based your self-diagnosis on an incomplete or inaccurate understanding of what constitutes a formal autism diagnosis, or there may have been some flaws in the assessment process which limited your ability to communicate all of the information necessary for the diagnostician to make an accurate assessment. The other possibility is that the diagnostician did not have sufficient experience and knowledge of adult autism, particularly of those who mask or have learned compensatory strategies, to 'see' your autism.

Self-diagnosis can be entirely adequate and valid for those who are confident in their own self-assessment and who need little or no external formal support which may require evidence of disability. Asking people why they have come for assessment often reveals a need for 'permission' or 'validation' from an external source that they trust. If the individual feels that their own assessment is enough and that the process of arriving at this conclusion gives them all they need personally, then diagnostic assessment has little value. Some people feel that a formal assessment gives them the confidence to disclose, as they are now 'official', and others have said that they don't feel comfortable joining groups for autistic people without a diagnosis, as they don't feel they have the right to be there.

If any form of care, financial aid, education, or employment support is required, either now or in the future, a formal diagnosis may well be required in order to provide medical evidence of the outcome. This will vary depending on individual circumstances, and many employers will take a person's word for it when they disclose a disability, but this is not always the case. We have met people who have been quite satisfied with their own self-diagnosis for a number of years, but whose circumstances have changed and who now need proof of their autistic status.

Clinical Diagnostic Processes

There is no single, standardized test for autism. There is also no genetic test, blood test, or brain scan that can identify autism. Therefore, a diagnosis of autism is, to some degree, subjective, and relies on not only the knowledge and skills of the diagnostician, but also accurate and full information being provided/requested. The diagnostic process is executed via an assessment interview between the client/patient and a diagnostician, and the outcome is generally given at the end of the interview or at some point later if several diagnosticians are involved.

In the absence of brain scans and blood tests, autism assessment focuses on behaviour and experiences throughout the lifespan, which support each element of the diagnostic criteria. This information is gathered via interview, observation, questionnaires, and/or clinical tools used to identify and evidence the presence of these autistic features.

The accuracy of the outcome depends on the ability of the diagnostician to interpret and apply the diagnostic criteria correctly and to elicit the information necessary for them to do this. The latter is particularly relevant in the case of adult autism diagnosis where early childhood history may not be available due to the lack of family members able to provide this, and also the learned strategies and masked behaviours which may make any autistic features less visible and obvious.

The processes involved in carrying out adult autism assessments vary across the world and are not standardized, even within the same country. In general, the DSM-5 and ICD-11 diagnostic criteria are followed, and as we have seen, these two sets are broadly similar in the elements required for a positive autism diagnostic outcome, which means that wherever you are in the world, what defines autism is fairly consistent, but how these criteria are applied is not. This can lead to great variability in outcome: a person being assessed by two different diagnosticians may receive two different outcomes – even within the same diagnostic service.

These differences in how the diagnostic criteria are applied, how diagnoses are tracked, availability of diagnosis, and cultural views of autism and disability mean that reported prevalence rates for autism vary widely worldwide. This may have relevance to you if you live in a country where autism education and diagnosis is low for economic, cultural, or other reasons. The countries with the highest rates of autism diagnosis are the UK, Sweden, Japan, and the USA with a diagnosis rate of around 70 in every 10,000 people. The countries with the lowest numbers of diagnoses are Taiwan, North Korea, Tunisia, Morocco, and India with around 30 in every 10,000 people having a diagnosis (www.wisevoter.com). Rates of diagnosis have increased significantly in recent years. In the USA, for example, according to The Centers for Disease Control (2023), 1:150 people were diagnosed in 2000 with this increasing to 1:44 in 2018. There are a number of opinions and views to explain this increase, but the most obvious one appears to be a greater awareness and knowledge of autism, along with a broadening of the presentation which is deemed to meet the criteria compared to the past when autism was seen as rare and only found among those with intellectual disabilities. The diagnostic criteria for Asperger syndrome – autism without accompanying intellectual disability, which has now been removed in name – was first included in the diagnostic criteria in 1994 and so it would be reasonable to expect that it would take time for people with this autistic profile to be seen and identified in large enough numbers to alter the stats.

In order to provide guidance regarding recommendations about how autism diagnostic assessments should be carried out, some countries have produced guidelines for this specifically for adults, and these are listed in the Resources section. For example, in the UK, there are the National Institute for Clinical Excellence (NICE) guidelines for Autism Spectrum Disorder in Adults: Diagnosis and

Management and in Australia, the Australia National Guideline for the Assessment and Diagnosis of ASD. The USA has no guidelines for the diagnosis of adults, only for children. France, Italy, and Spain have their own guidelines which can be found on the Autism Europe website, although some of these also only focus on the diagnosis of children but may give some insight as to what might be expected.

Guidance in what is considered to be the delivery of good quality autism diagnostic assessments typically advises on the following:

- Professionals involved should be trained and competent
- Early development and past historical information should be sought
- The purpose and process of the assessment and outcome should be explained at the start of the process
- Assessment should provide opportunities for observation and interaction – this can be online or in person

During the assessment itself, information should be gathered on the following:

- Core autistic features as listed in the DSM-5 or ICD-11 diagnostic criteria – this can be assessed using one of a number of clinical diagnostic tools or via informal interview
- Early developmental history – where this information is available – to include any speech or other developmental delays or differences, and support received (e.g., speech and language therapy)
- Behavioural or functional differences throughout the lifespan from childhood to present day – typically including education, employment, homelife, and social relationships
- History of mental health: anxiety and depression
- Other mental health diagnoses: schizophrenia, OCD etc.
- Other neurodevelopmental diagnosis: ADHD, dyslexia, tic disorder etc.
- Other relevant health conditions: hypermobility, PCOS etc.

- Family history: diagnosis of neurodevelopmental, mental, and other health conditions in family members

There are a number of clinical tools which some services use to supplement the assessment process, although these should not be used exclusively to make a diagnosis and should be part of a wider process which includes observation, developmental history, and interview. We provide an overview of the main clinical tools used for diagnosis. It should be noted that these are different from the screening tools previously mentioned, which are only used to determine whether an autism diagnostic assessment looks like a worthwhile pursuit. The following clinical instruments are designed for use as part of the assessment itself, rather than prior. Depending on the availability of autism assessment in your location and whether the assessment is via state healthcare or is privately funded, you may have no choice in which assessment method and clinical instruments are used. The following outlines of the most commonly used clinical tools are provided to give some idea of what might happen and how this might influence the outcome of your assessment.

The Autism Diagnostic Observation Schedule (ADOS)

The ADOS is delivered via semi-structured interview and observation. Clients are asked a series of questions and given various activities to complete under the observation of the assessor. It was developed in 1990 and continues to be updated and revised and has been translated into more than 19 languages. The ADOS is carried out by trained examiners and is based on the DSM criteria. Each diagnostic item is given a score of between 0 and 3 based on the 'severity' of the symptom as observed by the examiners. Scores from specific items form part of a series of algorithms which result in an outcome of either autism or no autism.

The Developmental, Dimensional, and Diagnostic Interview – Adult Version (3Di)

The 3Di is a structured interview based on items from the DSM-5 diagnostic criteria with items scored on a 0–3 or 0–4 scale. The questions are divided into sections A and B, with A focusing on social communication and interaction, and B on restricted, repetitive patterns of behaviour, interests, or activities. The outcome is calculated via the use of cut-off scores for both A and B. A score which exceeds the cut-off score in both sections A and B will result in a positive autism diagnostic outcome.

The Diagnostic Interview for Social and Communication Disorders (DISCO)

The DISCO takes the form of a semi-structured interview administered by a trained examiner. Rather than ratings only being derived from set questions, they can be given for any information provided by the examiner, individual, caregiver, or any other person. Along with the standard autism items, the DISCO also asks questions relating to attention and daily living among other non-diagnostic criteria specific items. It also provides an overall profile of both skills and challenges. Items are rated on a 3-point scale of severe, minor, or not present. Algorithms are used to generate the outcome based on these scores.

The Autism Diagnostic Interview – Revised (ADI-R)

The ADI-R is another semi-structured interview delivered by a trained clinician. Questions are based on developmental history and the current profile of the individual. Scores relating to historical items are derived from a specific age in childhood, or at the point where the behaviour was at its most atypical. Scoring is based on the administrator's opinion of the information provided, rather than that of the patient/client, and the outcome calculated by algorithms which dictate that cut-off scores across all domains must be met.

The above clinical instruments are the most commonly used and considered to have a high accuracy rate, but should not be used alone to generate a diagnostic outcome. Additional care should be taken if the individual being assessed has any additional differences which may potentially affect the accuracy of the tool due to additional communication challenges, a difficulty in isolating autistic features from other comorbid conditions, and the ability of the diagnostician to 'see' non-traditional autistic features in those who mask. These may include:

- Non-native speakers of the clinical instrument's language
- Females
- Those who do not identify as male
- Those who do not speak and communicate through the written word
- Those with severe anxiety
- Those with selective mutism
- Those with blindness, deafness, or physical disabilities
- Those with comorbid neurodevelopmental differences – ADHD, dyslexia etc.
- Those with comorbid mental health diagnoses – anxiety, schizophrenia, personality disorder

Other Diagnostic Methods

There are many diagnostic providers who do not use clinical instruments at all, or only as a small part of the decision making process. Others may use screening tools as part of their assessment process, rather than prior to it, as a means of gathering as big a picture as possible about the profile and experiences of the person seeking assessment, to ensure that the outcome is as accurate as it can be.

Regardless of whether clinical tools such as those listed above are used, most diagnostic assessments will involve the completion of a developmental questionnaire and a diagnostic interview, either in person or, more frequently these days, online.

Developmental Questionnaire

Most assessment services will ask the client to complete a questionnaire relating to their childhood history and ask questions focused on the diagnostic criteria in both childhood and adulthood. There is no standardized version of this questionnaire as they are usually developed in-house, but they are fairly similar in nature and the headings will be similar to those featured in the Notes and Thoughts section of the Appendix (towards the end of the book). You may be requested to return this questionnaire prior to the assessment interview so that the diagnostician can review it before the interview takes place. These questionnaires often ask for input from family members, particularly those who knew you as a child and may be able to give evidence that you yourself cannot remember or don't know. Some services will refuse to assess anyone who is unable to provide this information from a third party, which can be especially difficult for older people or those who have no family, are estranged from them, or who do not wish their family to know that they are undertaking autism assessment. Other services may request this information, but for them it is not obligatory. You will, however, be asked questions about your childhood to ascertain that autistic features have been present throughout your life, even though they may have manifested with more impact at some times more than others. It can be helpful to get some input from people who have known you in different settings and times in your life as they may have memories and observations which you do not and this can all provide valuable evidence for the assessment. However, it can also be the case that some people around you are resistant to the idea that you may be autistic due to their own lack of knowledge about how autism can present, and their input may not be congruent with your own experiences. For example, they may recall you being comfortable socially as a child, when you do not believe that this was actually the case: perhaps you were highly stressed but not showing it, or only spending time with peers who shared the same interests as you, where you dominated the relationship or conversation.

It is advisable to spend some time making notes and thinking of examples of how you meet the diagnostic criteria. You should be able to provide additional information that you consider to be relevant even if it is not directly asked for in the questions, and do not be afraid to do so – this is your assessment and you should be free to give your information in whatever quantity and format works best for you. Whilst many diagnosticians will have read your question-naire prior to the interview, some will not. They may prefer to read it during the interview and may ask you the same questions that you have already responded to in the questionnaire. You may wish to print out a copy or have one downloaded on your phone that you can refer to during the interview.

The Diagnostic Interview

All autism assessments will have some form of face-to-face (online or in-person) meeting(s) or interview(s) with one or more diagnosticians. Generally, this will be a single interview in the case of adults, but on occasion a second meeting may be required, either because this is the process used by the service or because a second opinion or further information is required in the case of an outcome not being clear after the initial meeting. You should be welcome to take someone along to the interview to support you and you can choose whether they remain in the room throughout the interview or only for parts of it, if you wish to speak privately to the diagnostician. You can decide whether you want the person accompanying you to take part in the assessment, or to remain quiet.

The interview typically takes between one and three hours and the likely length should be made clear to you prior to the meeting. You should also know how many people will be in the room, what their roles are and their names. The job titles and qualifications of the person/people who interview you may be varied and include mental health practitioners, clinical psychologists, occupational therapists, neurodevelopmental diagnosticians and others. They will all have been trained to carry out adult autism assessments and will have a range of experience and specialisms. It may be possible for you to carry out some research on the person who will assess you to gain some familiarity with what they look like and what their diagnostic experience is. It won't always be possible for you to do this in a state healthcare setting where there may be many diagnosticians working and many assessments taking place each day. In this case, you can just ask them about their qualifications and experience if you feel the need to do so. If you have been given a named person who you will see, you should also be informed in advance if for some reason this changes and you will see someone else. An autistic assessment service will be working with predominantly autistic clients and should provide a physical environment and communication approaches which make the experience as stress-free as possible for autistic people.

Depending on whether additional clinical tools are used and the style of the diagnostician, the interview may be more or less structured. A very structured interview will have fixed questions and a fixed format, which the diagnostician does not deviate from. A less structured interview may feel more informal and like a conversation, where the diagnostician asks questions and then supplementary questions based on your responses. The conversation may move from topic to topic, but the diagnostician will be taking notes and focusing their questions to gather the information that they need to evidence the diagnostic criteria. You may be less aware of this in this type of interview as the questions may be more nuanced.

Feel free to take notes to the interview as recalling information and examples when asked on the spot can be extremely difficult, especially if you are anxious about the interview and meeting a new person. You should be able to take a break during the interview if you need one, but be aware that the diagnostician may be under time constraints for their following appointments and may need to complete the interview in a fixed time period wherever possible.

If possible, keep the rest of the day free after your assessment as you will likely be exhausted by it. It can be an emotional experience sharing parts of your life openly in a way that you may not have done before, and being asked questions for up to three hours is draining for most people. The outcome itself may take some time to process if this is given at the time, so take care of yourself and allow yourself to rest, take a walk and let the experience settle in your mind as it could be one of the most important days of your life – this is certainly reported by many autistic people. More than one person has said that it was a more important day than the birth of their children.

The Outcome

Most diagnosticians will give you the outcome of the assessment immediately at the end of the interview, although those using clinical tools and a multi-disciplinary approach which involves more than one assessor or tests to be scored may not be able to do this. In this case you should be told when and how you will receive the outcome; whether by phone, email, or at a follow-up meeting. The outcome in most cases will be a simple Yes, you meet the diagnostic criteria for autism, or No, you don't. There may be an explanation of why this outcome has been reached and an opportunity to ask questions about this. You may be asked for your thoughts on the outcome and what it means for you. If the outcome is a shock to you, which can be the case, you may find it hard to think of any questions or process your reaction on the spot, and this is OK. You should be given the opportunity to ask further questions at a later date by email or telephone.

Depending on the service and assuming a positive autism outcome, there may be follow-up support available in the form of future post-diagnostic sessions to allow you to explore the new diagnosis once you have had time to process it. You may also be given or sent resources and information to allow you to learn more about your new diagnosis and how to best use it to support your life in the future. A diagnosis of autism is not the end of the journey – it is actually the beginning.

Whatever route you decide to take, it is important that the information that you base your initial self-assessment on is full and accurate and that, wherever possible, you select a diagnostician or service that has a good track record and reputation of diagnosing autistic adults.

Chapter 10

The Answer Is No, Now What?

You may want to skip this chapter if you have decided to self-identify as autistic, pursue an autism diagnosis, or have already been given one.

Not everyone who has an assessment is given a diagnosis, even if they are utterly convinced they are autistic. If you have been searching for answers to why you have always struggled and felt like an outsider, being told that you are not autistic is very likely to come as a rather unwelcome shock. You do still have options if you believe the diagnostician was wrong.

Alternatively, you may be relieved not to be autistic and to be able to eliminate autism from your enquiries and can now search for answers elsewhere.

There are a plethora of reasons for why you may not have got the diagnosis and some examples that we have heard include:

- You do not meet the diagnostic criteria – this is the most simple and obvious reason

However, if you were expecting an autistic outcome, here are some other reasons which may explain this:

- A diagnostician with limited experience of adults, females and those who mask conducted the assessment
- You are subclinical – you are deemed to have autistic traits but not enough to give the diagnosis
- Not enough childhood information
- The diagnostic tool used was inappropriate (the ADOS-2 seems to be the most common)
- Your levels of masking during the appointment meant that your autistic self could not be 'seen' by the clinician
- Being able to maintain eye contact
- Having a reciprocal conversation with the diagnostician
- Other neurodivergent, mental health, or physical conditions masking the autism (diagnosed or undiagnosed)

As mentioned earlier in this book, there is no standardized test for autism and it cannot be detected by scans or blood tests. That means that the outcome depends on how the diagnostician applies the criteria and their opinion on how you have presented this evidentially during the assessment; it is therefore a highly subjective process. If you have not been given the diagnosis on the basis of insufficient childhood (or any other) evidence, trying to get more input from family members, a lifelong friend, or someone very close to you will likely help.

There is also the possibility that you are not actually autistic, which is also something that you will need to consider – more on that in a bit.

If you do disagree with the outcome you will have to decide whether or not a second opinion and going through the process all over again is worth it for you. The first assessment may have been too traumatizing for you to want to put yourself through it again, you may have lost faith in the clinical route, or you just do not have the funds to go private. If you decide not to, you will then need to make the choice to just move on from the idea of autism altogether or decide to self-identify as autistic. Whether or not you decide to get a second opinion, ask for the assessment report and a follow-up meeting to go over the results and why the criteria were not met.

There is a slim chance at this point that you may be able to explain why you answered some of the questions in the way you did, which could shift the outcome.

If you have decided that seeking a second opinion is the best route for you, you should first approach the team that initially assessed you. Although there are no guarantees that a reassessment will come back with a different outcome, you may decide that this is worth pursuing, especially if you have new information which may address some of the parts of the diagnostic criteria that were deemed not to have been met previously. If you are in a country with state healthcare, such as the UK, you can ask to be referred elsewhere for a second opinion. In England, the Right to Choose scheme mentioned previously allows individuals to choose the provider for their mental health services, which includes autism diagnostic assessments. This can reduce typical wait times from up to four years to just a few months.

The alternative is that you seek an assessment privately. You will have to pay for this yourself, and again there are no guarantees that you will get the outcome that you hope for. If you decide to see a private diagnostician, make sure you do your due diligence, get recommendations from others, and only go with a provider that you are happy with. The cost of autism assessments varies widely in price and the fee may not necessarily reflect the qualifications and experience of the assessor. If you do need/want a clinical diagnosis, check which professionals are allowed to offer these in your country. You do not want to be in the position of finally getting a 'yes, you're autistic' and then not being able to use it for state benefits, support, or work/education purposes. There are also people offering non-clinical autism assessments for those that do not need a clinical diagnosis, but still do your research as to their reputation and experience in carrying out these assessments. It is very unlikely that healthcare providers, benefits agencies, employers, or educational institutions will accept a non-clinical assessment report as proof of an autism diagnosis.

You may also want to consider how you will feel after a second assessment if the outcome is that you are autistic – some people feel confused by the conflicting outcomes of two assessments. If you are unsure how you will process this it may be best to speak to someone who has experience in supporting people through autism assessments, like a mentor or coach.

It is important to note here that if you get multiple negative autism outcomes from different professionals there will come a point in which you will need to accept that the likelihood is that you are not meeting the threshold for the diagnostic criteria. This may be difficult to accept at first, if you felt strongly that you would, but if there is consistent evidence that you do not meet the criteria, then autism may not be the answer for you and you may need to move on. This will also be the case if you have gone through this book and scored yourself very low at the end of each chapter, or you have discovered that your differences are not due to autism but something else (so all is not lost).

If you feel that you are not autistic but there is something else that warrants investigation, it may be worth revisiting Chapter 6, What Else Could It Be? If one or more of the conditions outlined resonated with you, it will be worthwhile doing some more thorough research. Once you feel confident that something else is a better fit, the next step would then be to approach your GP and ask for a referral for an assessment, or look into a private one.

Try to look at the positives of ruling out autism. It means that you can start to look at other possibilities for your differences/difficulties, which may offer a better explanation and more helpful support strategies. If autism isn't the answer then something else might be. If you try to adopt autism-specific coping mechanisms and strategies when you are not autistic, the chances are they will not be overly helpful.

Chapter 11

It's a Yes, Now What?

BEYOND (SELF-)DIAGNOSIS

Whether you have chosen to self-identify as autistic or seek a clinical diagnosis, you may be wondering what to do now. How do you live your best autistic life? Who do you tell and when? What support is out there?

Emotions Post-Diagnosis/Self-Identifying

Whatever your emotions are at this stage, please be assured that they are completely valid.

Everyone feels differently once they have been told they are autistic or have come to this realization alone. You may go through different emotions including grief, denial, and anger, but hopefully you will end with acceptance and empowerment. Over time, you should come to accept that being autistic is not negative, it is just an explanation for why you have always felt like you do not quite fit into this neurotypical world. With this explanation you can start to make changes in your life, if you feel it necessary, so that you can start to live the best life possible for you.

Your journey to acceptance may not be linear, and may bounce back and forth between different emotions. Post-diagnosis imposter syndrome is extremely common. You may wonder if you tricked the diagnostician into giving you the diagnosis, or if you're self-diagnosed may feel that you have made it all up and therefore cannot claim that you are autistic to the wider world. Anecdotally, there is also a phenomenon where people feel like they have become 'more' autistic than they have ever been before. If this is something that you have experienced, we guarantee that you haven't become more autistic, you are just more aware of how you are reacting to the world around you. You may also be allowing the mask to slip and no longer forcing yourself to do the things that have always had a negative impact on you. It can take time to fully give yourself permission to unmask and unleash your full autistic self on the world.

One phrase that we hear often is 'Why did nobody spot this sooner?' The answer to this, in short, is that you are very likely to have slipped under the radar due to being able to fit in just enough. The cost of this has probably been high to you but unfortunately this is seldom noticed by others. There has also been a huge amount more research and therefore, in more recent times, a better understanding of how being autistic may present differently than originally thought. What is also important to remember is that the majority of participants in early research studies were male children.

Disclosure

There is no right or wrong time to disclose that you are autistic. This is your new piece of information about yourself, and it is for you to tell who you want and when you want. Once it is out there, you cannot take it back or control what others do with it or how they respond, and unfortunately sometimes people react in ways you may not want them to. For you this may be the most exciting and positive thing that has happened for a long time, and you may find yourself wanting to talk about it all the time. For those close to you, it may be uninteresting, or at worst they may have a predisposed idea of autism and you do not fit it. We have all heard stories of people disclosing and being told, 'You don't look autistic', 'You can't be because you have a job/ partner/children', 'But you like people and autistic people don't', and, maybe the most common, 'We're all a little bit autistic'.

Regardless of who you are telling, the best place to start is deciding what information you would like to disclose. You do not have to be the flag bearer for autism if you do not want to. If you do, fantastic. There can never be too many autistic voices in the world sharing their lived experiences. However, if the thought of putting yourself out there on social media, shouting about it from the rooftops, fills you with horror, that is OK too.

You may have people ask you where you are on the spectrum. Remember that the spectrum is not linear.

You may hear autistic people being described as high or low functioning, which, within the autistic community, is not seen as helpful and you may have to educate those close to you if they are guilty of doing this. The reason for this is because it places the onus on the individual and does not take into consideration the impact that the environment has on them. It also takes away the daily struggles for people who are considered high functioning, and also doesn't give credit to people who are considered low functioning who do have a wealth of skills but which may not be deemed as such in general society, for example, someone who has phenomenal art skills but is non-speaking or cannot live independently.

It is really important to remember, for example, your sensory differences may be more heightened after a day of socializing and being out in the world than they would be if you had stayed at home. Your capacity to socialize may be less after spending all day at work or with the children. This is the main reason that we should not use functioning language (less, a little bit, really, severely etc.).

Another question you may want to prepare yourself for is 'How does being autistic affect you?' For this, we could split autism down into its key parts:

- Social – friends, family, colleagues, relationships
- Communication – use and understanding of language both formally and informally
- Flexibility, routines, and change
- Interests
- Sensory

Then come up with an example of how you meet the criteria. As an example, Jess has written how she would explain about being autistic to others. It is useful to prepare some responses in advance rather than feeling put on the spot when people ask.

Social

I find eye contact really difficult and tend to look around all the time. I enjoy socializing but need a lot of people-free time as well. If you have an emotional problem I am very good at finding a solution for you, but may not offer comfort or a hug.

Communication

I take jokes and sarcasm literally and have an urge to correct people when they are wrong. I can monologue and not realize that someone is bored. I often have to ask people if they are OK as I struggle to pick up on non-verbal cues.

Routines and Change

Lists, lists, lists! I have a list for everything and I am good at planning. Certain tasks, like loading the dishwasher, have systems and other people just do it wrong! I can be very set in my opinions and need a lot of evidence that I am wrong about something.

Interests

I have many interests, some are shorter lived than others. I love learning and researching new topics. These have included pottery, knitting, baking, and lino printing.

Sensory

I wear sunglasses all year round due to being very sensitive to light. I often wear noise cancelling headphones, both inside and outside the house. I cannot stand the texture of certain foods and hate tomatoes. I seek out other textures such as fizzy drinks.

It shouldn't all be negative and do not feel that you have to go deep into your personal life. After all, it's not really anyone else's business. You may feel the need to change parts the more you tell people, depending on reactions you get, but over time, what you say is likely to become almost script-like. Once you have decided how much information you are happy to share, you can start approaching people.

Important Things to Remember

- Only tell people you want to, feel you have to, or feel safe to
- Do not share more than you are comfortable with
- You get to say no. Do not feel pressured into sharing anything that you do not want to

Telling Your Family and Friends

Telling people that you are close to may be the best place to start as they are more likely to be accepting of your news. Some people decide to disclose to friends and family that they are investigating whether or not they are autistic before they have even been assessed. The benefit of this is hopefully not feeling alone after your assessment. Others decide that they want to keep it to themselves until they have confirmation. Again, there is no hard and fast rule, it is all about what you feel comfortable with.

Writing a letter or an email may help you map out exactly what you would like to say to them. You could find and share a video clip from YouTube or TikTok created by an autistic person that accurately describes your experience and who has expressed it particularly well. Sometimes, when people hear information from a source that is one step removed from you and from an 'expert', it can be easier for them to process and accept it as being valid. If this diagnosis is positive for you, make sure that you make this clear to people. There is still a lot of stigma around being autistic and the only way to break this is to explain what being autistic means to you. Unfortunately, a lot of discussions around autism are about what people cannot do rather than what they excel in. Focus on your strengths, and when talking about your difficulties, come up with suggestions of how your family and friends can support you. Also make sure you state your boundaries very clearly about who you are happy for friends and family members to tell – if it is no one, make that crystal clear. Reiterate that this is about your personal life and you're sure that they wouldn't want you to tell everyone about theirs. It is the same and people need to respect your wishes.

Telling Your Employer

It is important to remember that, in the UK, you do not legally have to tell your current or any future employers that you are autistic until you want or it is necessary to. Please check what the local laws are if you are outside of the UK. When disclosing to employers, discuss specifically how your job is influenced by being autistic and what impact this is having on you, especially if it affects your mental or physical health. This may include the physical environment that you work in, the communication and management culture, and the procedures and pace of the organization. You should also emphasize the positive aspects of being autistic in your role, such as your attention to detail and knowledge of the industry that you work in.

Depending on the disability laws in your country, or, in the absence of these, your employer's willingness to implement strategies to support you, various possible adjustments may be helpful:

- Working environment – changing light bulbs, being seated away from the noise and smells of the kitchen
- Working arrangements – flexible working hours, working from home, hybrid working (part at home, part in the office)
- Communication support – written rather than verbal instructions, not being interrupted, advance warning of impending changes
- Providing support and equipment – autism awareness training for staff/managers, specialist support workers/mentors, antiglare screens, specialist chairs
- Finding an alternative approach to accomplish your work – being given extra time to do certain tasks, providing information in a different format, meeting agendas in advance

These are just some ideas and there are many other reasonable adjustments that you can ask for, either in work or when applying for a job. What job you do and what you find challenging will determine what adjustments will be suitable for you. Employers can refuse adjustments if they are not cost effective, cause too many disruptions to the business, or if they change the nature of the job beyond the scope of which you were employed.

Medical Professionals

Any medical professional that you come into contact with is likely to need proof of your diagnosis, if gained privately and not via your local healthcare system. It can be helpful to tell your doctor if you are in need of some adjustments made to your care or if you are speaking to them about a co-occurring condition such as ADHD, anxiety, or depression. Some of the common co-occurring conditions were discussed in an earlier chapter.

Framework for an Autistic Life

Once you have assimilated the new knowledge of being autistic, the next steps are to make adjustments to your own life. What constitutes a good life will vary for everyone, and when making changes, it is important to start small and make sure they are achievable. If you break each change down into manageable pieces, and tackle each one at a time instead of all at once, you are much more likely to succeed. Think about people making New Year's resolutions – they decide that they are going to make massive changes in all areas of their lives such as getting a new job, exercising, eating healthily, saving money. However, a week or two into their life-overhaul, 'new year, new me', they become completely overwhelmed by trying to do everything at once, and end up giving it all up and reverting back to their normal life. By starting off small you can build strong foundations and if you have a good solid base then you will not feel burdened by what you are trying to achieve.

The first hurdle is to make sure you are focusing your time, effort, and energy optimally. There are certain things that every human being needs in order to survive and provide for people who are dependent on them. These are the 'need to do' – food, hydration, sleep, shelter, and income (think Maslow's hierarchy of needs; 1943). In this day and age, we also have a lot of life admin that needs to be kept on top of. So your 'need to do' list includes all the tasks that you cannot escape from, including paying the bills!

Next we move on to all the things that we think we should be doing, which will be different for everyone. Autistic people can end up putting a lot of pressure on themselves to conform to neuronormative conventions and ways of living. The shoulds are the ones that people force themselves to do and are more likely to cause harm in the long term. It may be to keep up a big social circle you have to mask heavily, which in turn can be exhausting. Considering how many of the shoulds are actually healthy and valuable to you can be a cathartic experience as you build your autistic life and choose to possibly discard some of them that no longer meet your needs (or perhaps never did).

Finally, the want-to-do. These should be all the things that bring you that amazing autistic joy, which is different for everyone. They could be based around interests, the people you want to spend your time with, education, career progression, or sitting in bed binge watching your favourite TV shows. After the need-to-do, these should be your priority.

It is important to work these out so that your energy is focused on the tasks and activities that you need to do and want to do. This is the first step to setting out a framework that meets your individual needs. If there are tasks that you struggle with but fall into the 'need to' category, you may want to consider asking for help from people around you, or look into mentoring, coaching, or therapy. If you are not doing so already, start to manage your time so that you do not overwhelm yourself on a daily basis. Map out all of your responsibilities and the things that you want to do so that you can start to come up with plans and routines that do not put you in an energy deficit. There are online resources that talk about energy accounting, spoon theory, and ticket theory. Professor Tony Attwood and autistic clinical psychologist Maja Toudal have written an excellent workbook to assist with this process of managing energy (Attwood and Toudal, 2024). All of these are, in essence, slightly different takes on the same thing. In a nutshell, you have a set amount of spoons/credits/tickets per day, and each task you do uses up a certain amount of energy. For example, you may have 20 spoons/credits/tickets per day, and commuting takes up 2, work 10, cooking 2, food shop 3, and chores 3 – leaving you with nothing spare. Some days you will have energy left over to take into the next, other days you will be in an energy deficit (try not to have too many of these days). Once you have figured out how much energy tasks take up, you can then start to work out what gives you back the energy and factor this into your day.

Another useful way to adjust your life is to take stock of your sensory environment and carry out a sensory audit. As we know, many autistic people face an onslaught from the sensory world on a daily basis. They may be hypersensitive (needing less input), hyposensitive (needing more input), or a mixture of both. Even though everyone's sensory profile is different, the commonality is that autistic people have sensory needs. Dr Luke Beardon's equation, Autism + Environment = Outcome (2017, p. 11), is a good framework to try to live by. In short, if the environment (internal and external) suits your individual needs, your outcomes are more likely to be positive (outcomes can be absolutely anything).

One way to achieve this is to carry out a sensory profile or audit of places that you spend large amounts of time in. A good place to start is at home. You may need to do one for different environments as the sensory aspect of them may change depending on where you are. Having control is the key to managing your sensory needs. Although you can't control everything that goes on around you, you can make small changes to manage the environment to best suit you and come up with strategies that help.

There are the obvious main sensory categories – light, noise, touch, smell, taste, as well as interoception. This is the ability to understand what your body needs. Some autistic people can struggle to pick up signals such as when they need to eat, drink, or go to the bathroom.

Once you have analysed what your sensory needs are, it's time to get creative. In the table below, there are some suggestions that may help with each specific need. Some of these may seem obvious.

What to Include in a Sensory Audit

Start by considering what your main sensory differences are. Here are some examples:

Sight:	Sound:
• I do not like bright lights • I prefer natural lighting • I need total darkness to sleep • I find certain colours are calming	• I prefer loud sounds • I prefer quiet sounds • I prefer complete silence • I like loud sounds when I am in control of them (i.e., music)
Taste – food/drinks:	**Touch – clothing/materials:**
• I like spicy foods • I don't like slimy textures • I like crunchy textures • I do not like unexpected textures • Food can/cannot touch • I have to use certain cutlery/mugs/glasses/crockery • I can only have certain shaped pasta/brand of foods	• I do not like scratchy materials/labels in clothes • I do not like tight clothes • I like soft materials **Touch – people:** • I prefer light touch • I do not like to be touched • I prefer firm touch
Smell:	**Interoception:**
• I do not like strong perfumes • I love certain smells • Some smells give me a headache • Some smells make me feel unwell • Some smells make me feel calm	• When focused I forget to eat • I do not know when I am thirsty • I often do not realize I need the toilet until I am desperate

Once you have figured out your sensory profile, think of ways to manage these needs and preferences. Again, here are some examples:

Sight:	Sound:
• Carry sunglasses • Change ceiling light bulbs • Only use lamps • Buy coloured string lights • Buy blackout blinds or curtains	• Use noise-cancelling headphones • Spend time in quiet spaces throughout the day • Listen to music/podcasts when out

Taste – food/drinks:	Touch – clothing/materials:
• Come up with a weekly food plan • Always have fizzy drinks at home • Only buy one brand of cereal • Check menus online before visiting restaurants • Take your own food with you when going to work or out for the day	• Take out all labels in clothes • Throw out woollen jumpers • Only buy cotton clothing **Touch – people:** • Get weighted blanket • Set boundaries with people • Book a massage
Smell:	**Interoception:**
• Replace toiletries for fragrant free ones • Get rid of all air fresheners • Carry material with favourite smell on	• Set alarms to remind me to drink/eat • Ask people to remind me to drink/eat • Do hourly 'body needs' check-in – am I hungry/thirsty/needing the toilet?

Then start to put everything in place. It can take some time to form new habits but it will be worth it in the long run.

Seeking Support – Peers Groups/Therapy/Mentoring/Coaching

You may be completely happy to navigate post-diagnosis alone and without the input of a professional, but for a lot of people they find it helpful to talk to someone so they can start to unpick life – both past, present, and future. Therapy tends to focus a lot on the past and how that impacts you now, along with emotions, whereas mentoring and coaching approaches are more practical or education based, helping to make changes for now and the future. In Steph Jones' book *The Autistic Survival Guide to Therapy*, she believes that when seeking support it is most helpful when there is a good connection with the therapist, psychoeducation, and a dual approach of therapy and coaching (Jones, 2024, pp. 200–201).

Whatever form of support you decide to engage in, you will need to be open about your neurotype so that they can help you.

Remember that everything you do, think, and feel is because you are autistic. Fundamentally, autism comes first as it is how your brain works. If you also identify with having alexithymia, you should disclose this as well. A lot of therapists will ask you how you feel about a situation which is likely to be something that you will find very difficult to answer. It is important that the therapist, coach, or mentor has an understanding of autism. There are many autistic/neurodivergent therapists around the world and it may help to seek out one of them as they will have a much better insight into what it is like to be autistic. They are less likely to be dismissive and you may form a better connection with them. With so many professionals working online now that you are no longer limited by locality, pick the person that is right for you; this may take several goes. As with most things in life, finding the right support may be a case of trial and error. It does not mean that you cannot be helped, it just means you haven't yet found the right person. Another option is peer support groups which tend to be run by autistic people, for autistic people. They can be a great place to meet other autistic people at different stages of their autism discovery. There are many types out there that can be attended both in person and online. Some peer support groups are about autism in general, whereas others focus on the intersectionality between being autistic and a parent, gender identity, or sexuality. Other groups will be based around an activity such as art, music, walking, or sports. A lot of peer support groups also invite guest speakers to talk about a wide range of autism-related topics. Regardless of the secondary focus of the group, they provide an opportunity for people to be able to learn from each other by sharing their own experiences in an inclusive and supportive setting. The best place to find local peer support groups is on social media or through your country's autism charity/society. Some of these are listed in the Resources section at the end of the book.

Chapter 12

Final Words

This is the end... or perhaps the beginning.

And thus, dear reader, we have come to the end of our journey through the exploration of your, or that of someone close to you, potential autisticness, autisticability, or autisticity (I'm just making up words now).

We hope that at the very least you have learned something about yourself, about autism, autistic people, and maybe people in general. Perhaps you are now pretty convinced that you are autistic and are considering your next steps either towards assessment, or are satisfied with your own self-diagnosis. If so, congratulations and welcome to the gang. Your work now begins in identifying what to do next and how to tweak your life to keep well and have space for joy.

As we have tried to reiterate throughout this book there is no right or wrong way to process the realization that you are autistic. For some it may take time to adjust to the diagnosis and what it means for you, and you may need outside support. Others will jump for joy and move on with their lives.

Just be kind to yourself as you start to unpick all of those years of feeling like the weird one, the odd one out, the imposter in the world. You've got this.

Perhaps this book has led you to continue to question whether you are autistic or to be fairly sure that you are not, or that any traits that you may have would be unlikely to meet the requirements of the diagnostic criteria or are better explained by some other label. Maybe you have new leads to consider in other conditions or aspects of your profile that may take you towards another explanation for whatever brought you to this book in the first place. Hopefully you have learned something, found some answers, and have a new path to follow. We wish you well on your continued quest.

Maybe you still don't know what or who you are. Maybe none of the labels and explanations quite fit, and that is frustrating, because you can't get closure. In this case, you have the choice as to whether to keep on looking, find the closest match, and live by that, or simply stop looking and accept the unique self that you are. It may be that your profile is a comorbid one where autism, ADHD, dyslexia, or other neurodivergent conditions distort and dilute your profile, and you don't meet any of the criteria entirely. In this case, you may consider having an assessment which can identify all of the possible conditions that you present. Ultimately, the benefit of a diagnosis – self or otherwise – is to gain access to support strategies that work for you. If autistic, or any other condition, support approaches work for you, use them, regardless of whether you are diagnosed or not – no one is checking.

We live in a world where awareness and acceptance of diversity has never been greater. It may not always feel that way, and the degree of this will vary depending on where you happen to reside, but for the most part, it is the truth. Social media, online communities, and the internet have enabled people to gain knowledge, share experiences, and find support. Whatever difference you feel in yourself has a community of like-minded people out there, whether online or in person, and you can find them. There is no need to feel alone – reach out and find your people, wherever and whoever they may be.

The process of recognizing, exploring, and finding the name for who and what you are can be liberating and transformative, but also disorientating and upsetting, as you discover your true identity for the first time and consider how to live your best life going forward. The emotional journey may be a little rough at times, but this will settle in time, as this new self-perception becomes your new normal. Take care of yourself through this transition, take things slowly as it all sinks in, and don't make any big decisions that you may come to regret at a later time.

Wherever you now find yourself on your journey of self-discovery, just remember that none of this means that you are broken or wrong, and even if there is no official diagnostic label for what and who you are, that doesn't matter; you're OK as you are. We are all OK as we are.

References

Introduction

Sacks, O. (1995). *An Anthropologist on Mars: Seven Paradoxical Tales.* New York: Alfred A. Knopf.

Chapter 1 – What Exactly Is Autism?

American Psychiatric Association (APA). (2013). *Diagnostic and Statistical Manual of Mental Disorders, 5th edition* (DSM-5). APA.

World Health Organization (WHO). (2022). *International Classification of Diseases, Version 11* (ICD-11). WHO.

Chapter 2 – Diagnostic Features of Autism in the Real World

Attwood, A. (2008). *The Complete Guide to Asperger's Syndrome.* Jessica Kingsley Publishers.

Bogdashina, O. (2016). *Sensory Perceptual Issues in Autism and Asperger Syndrome, 2nd edition.* Jessica Kingsley Publishers.

Brang, D., & Ramachandran, V.S. (2011). Survival of the synesthesia gene: Why do people hear colors and taste words? *PLoS Biology*, 9(11), e1001205. https://doi.org/10.1371/journal.pbio.1001205

Fletcher-Watson, S., & Bird, G. (2019). Autism and empathy: What are the real links? *Autism*, 24(1), 3–6. https://doi.org/10.1177/1362361319883506

Howard, P.L., & Sedgewick, F. (2021). 'Anything but the phone!': Communication mode preferences in the autism community. *Autism*, 25(8), 2265–2278. https://doi.org/10.1177/13623613211014995

Hull, L., Mandy, W., Lai, M., Baron-Cohen, S., Allison, C., Smith, P., & Petrides, K.V. (2018). Development and validation of the Camouflaging Autistic Traits Questionnaire (CAT-Q). *Journal of Autism and Developmental Disorders*, 49(3), 819–833. https://doi.org/10.1007/s10803-018-3792-6

Lai, M., Lombardo, M.V., Ruigrok, A.N., Chakrabarti, B., Auyeung, B., Szatmari, P., Happé, F., & Baron-Cohen, S. (2016). Quantifying and exploring camouflaging in men and women with autism. *Autism*, 21(6), 690–702. https://doi.org/10.1177/1362361316671012

Livingston, L.A., Shah, P., & Happé, F. (2019). Compensatory strategies below the behavioural surface in autism: A qualitative study. *The Lancet Psychiatry*, 6(9), 766–777. https://doi.org/10.1016/s2215-0366(19)30224-x

Miller, D., Rees, J., & Pearson, A. (2021). 'Masking is life': Experiences of masking in autistic and nonautistic adults. *Autism in Adulthood*, 3(4), 330–338. https://doi.org/10.1089/aut.2020.0083

Milton, D.E. (2012). On the ontological status of autism: The 'double empathy problem'. *Disability & Society*, 27(6), 883–887. https://doi.org/10.1080/09687599.2012.710008

Simner, J., Mulvenna, C., Sagiv, N., Tsakanikos, E., Witherby, S.A., Fraser, C., Scott, K., & Ward, J. (2006). Synaesthesia: The prevalence of atypical cross-modal experiences. *Perception*, 35(8), 1024–1033. https://doi.org/10.1068/p5469

Chapter 3 – What Brings You Here?

Attwood, T. (2008). *The Complete Guide to Asperger Syndrome*. Jessica Kingsley Publishers.

Haddon, M. (2003). *The Curious Incident of the Dog in the Night-Time*. Jonathan Cape.

Ingudomnukul, E., Baron-Cohen, S., Wheelwright, S., & Knickmeyer, R. (2007). Elevated rates of testosterone-related disorders in women with autism spectrum conditions. *Hormones and Behavior*, 51(5), 597–604. doi:10.1016/j.yhbeh.2007.02.001.

Moseley, R., & Gamble-Turner, J. (2026) Autistic Menopause: A Guide to the Menopausal Transition for Autistic People and those Supporting Them. Jessica Kingsley Publishers.

Simantov, T., Pohl, A., Tsompanidis, A., Weir, E., et al. (2022). Medical symptoms and conditions in autistic women. *Autism*, 26(2), 373–388. doi:10.1177/13623613211022091.

Tinsley, M., & Hendrickx, S. (2008). *Asperger Syndrome and Alcohol: Drinking to Cope?* Jessica Kingsley Publishers.

Chapter 4 – I Can't Be Autistic Because...

American Psychiatric Association (APA). (2013). *Diagnostic and Statistical Manual of Mental Disorders, 5th edition* (DSM-5). APA.

Doherty, M., Johnson, M., & Buckley, C. (2021). Supporting autistic doctors in primary care: Challenging the myths and misconceptions. *British Journal of General Practice*, 71(708), 294–295. https://doi.org/10.3399/bjgp21X716165

Hendrickx, S. (2014). *Women and Girls on the Autism Spectrum*. Jessica Kingsley Publishers.

Jolly, J. (2022, November 22). Neurodivergent women sought for jobs at GCHQ and BAE Systems. *The Guardian*. www.theguardian.com/society/2022/nov/16/neurodiverse-women-sought-for-jobs-at-gchq-and-bae-systems

Milton, D. (2012). On the ontological status of autism: The 'double empathy problem'. *Disability and Society*, 27(3), 883–887.

Novellie, P. (2024). *Why Can't I Just Enjoy Things?* Blink Publishing.

Silvertant, E. (2023). *The Different Types of Empathy*. Embrace Autism. https://embrace-autism.com/the-different-types-of-empathy/

Chapter 5 – Supporting Evidence

Adamson, J., Brede, J., Babb, C., Serpell, L., Jones, J., Fox, J., & Mandy, W. (2022). Towards identifying a method of screening for autism amongst women with restrictive eating disorders. *European Eating Disorders Review*, 30. doi:10.1002/erv.2918.

Attanasio, M., Masedu, F., Quattrini, F., Pino, M.C., et al. (2022). Are autism spectrum disorder and asexuality connected? *Archives of Sexual Behavior*, 51(4), 2091–2115. doi:10.1007/s10508-021-02177-4.

Besag, F. (2017). Epilepsy in patients with autism: Links, risks and treatment challenges. *DOAJ (Directory of Open Access Journals)*. https://doaj.org/article/18331912c70c4bbd9302123d9b6c38bf

Buckley, A.W., Rodriguez, A.J., Jennison, K., Buckley, J., Thurm, A., Sato, S., & Swedo, S. (2010). Rapid eye movement sleep percentage in children with autism compared with children with developmental delay and typical development. *Archives of Pediatrics and Adolescent Medicine*, 164(11). https://doi.org/10.1001/archpediatrics.2010.202

Cherskov, A., Pohl, A., Allison, C., Zhang, H., Payne, R.A., & Baron-Cohen, S. (2018). Polycystic ovary syndrome and autism: A test of the prenatal sex steroid theory. *Translational Psychiatry*, 8(1). https://doi.org/10.1038/s41398-018-0186-7

Dewinter, J., De Graaf, H., & Begeer, S. (2017). Sexual orientation, gender identity, and romantic relationships in adolescents and adults with autism spectrum disorder. *Journal of Autism and Developmental Disorders*, 47(9), 2927–2934. doi:10.1007/s10803-017-3199-9.

Ehlers-Danlos Support UK. (2024). *Types of EDS – The Ehlers-Danlos Support UK*. www.ehlers-danlos.org/what-is-eds/information-on-eds/types-of-eds

Goldman, S.E., Alder, M.L., Burgess, H.J., Corbett, B.A., Hundley, R., Wofford, D., Fawkes, D.B., Wang, L., Laudenslager, M.L., & Malow, B.A. (2017). Characterizing sleep in adolescents and adults with autism spectrum disorders. *Journal of Autism and Developmental Disorders*, 47(6), 1682–1695. https://doi.org/10.1007/s10803-017-3089-1

Grant, S., Norton, S., Weiland, R.F., Scheeren, A.M., Begeer, S., & Hoekstra, R.A. (2022). Autism and chronic ill health: An observational study of symptoms and diagnoses of central sensitivity syndromes in autistic adults. *Molecular Autism*, 13(1). https://doi.org/10.1186/s13229-022-00486-6

Grant, S.L., Hoekstra, R., & Norton, S. (2025). Central sensitivity symptoms and autistic traits in Autistic and Non-Autistic adults. *Autism Research*. https://doi.org/10.1002/aur.3297

Hisle-Gorman, E., Landis, C.A., Susi, A., Schvey, N.A., et al. (2019). Gender dysphoria in children with autism spectrum disorder. *LGBT Health*, 6(3), 95–100. https://doi.org/10.1089/lgbt.2018.0252

IAPMD. (2024). FAQ – How many people with PMDD also have ADHD or autism? https://faq.iapmd.org/en/articles/7004494-how-many-people-with-pmdd-also-have-adhd-or-autism

Kiriakopoulos, E., & Obsorne Shafer, P. (2019). *Absence seizures*. www.epilepsy.com/what-is-epilepsy/seizure-types/absence-seizures#What-do-absence-seizures-look-like?

Madra, M., Ringel, R., & Margolis, K.G. (2020). Gastrointestinal issues and autism spectrum disorder. *Child and Adolescent Psychiatric Clinics of North America*, 29(3), 501–513. doi:10.1016/j.chc.2020.02.005.

McLean, K.J., Eack, S.M., & Bishop, L. (2021). The impact of sleep quality on quality of life for autistic adults. *Research in Autism Spectrum Disorders*, 88, 101849. https://doi.org/10.1016/j.rasd.2021.101849

MIND. (n.d.). *Symptoms of PMDD*. www.mind.org.uk/information-support/types-of-mental-health-problems/premenstrual-dysphoric-disorder-pmdd/symptoms-of-pmdd

National Autistic Society. (2017). *Epilepsy and Autism*. www.autism.org.uk/advice-and-guidance/professional-practice/epilepsy-autism

National Autistic Society. (2021). *Good Practice Guide for Professionals Delivering Talking Therapies for Autistic Adults and Children*. https://s2.chorus-mk.thirdlight.com/file/24/asDKIN9as.klK7easFDsalAzTC/NAS-Good-Practice-Guide-A4.pdf

Neumeyer, A.M., Anixt, J., Chan, J., Perrin, J.M., Murray, D., Coury, D.L., Bennett, A., Farmer, J., & Parker, R.A. (2018). Identifying associations among co-occurring medical conditions in children with autism spectrum disorders. *Academic Pediatrics*, 19(3), 300–306. https://doi.org/10.1016/j.acap.2018.06.014

NHS. (2024). *Fibromyalgia*. www.nhsinform.scot/illnesses-and-conditions/brain-nerves-and-spinal-cord/chronic-pain/fibromyalgia/

Obaydi, H., & Puri, B. (2008). Prevalence of premenstrual syndrome in autism: A prospective observer-rated study. *Journal of International Medical Research*, 36(2), 268–272. https://doi.org/10.1177/147323000803600208

Pohl, A.L., Crockford, S.K., Blakemore, M. et al. (2020). A comparative study of autistic and non-autistic women's experience of motherhood. *Molecular Autism*, 11, 3. https://doi.org/10.1186/s13229-019-0304-2

Raymaker, D.M., Teo, A.R., Steckler, N.A., Lentz, B., Scharer, M., Santos, A.D., Kapp, S.K., Hunter, M., Joyce, A., & Nicolaidis, C. (2020). 'Having all of your internal resources exhausted beyond measure and being left with no clean-up crew': Defining autistic burnout. *Autism in Adulthood*, 2(2), 132–143. https://doi.org/10.1089/aut.2019.0079.

Schreck, K.A., & Richdale, A.L. (2019). Sleep problems, behavior, and psychopathology in autism: Inter-relationships across the lifespan. *Current Opinion in Psychology*, 34, 105–111. https://doi.org/10.1016/j.copsyc.2019.12.003

Spiers, J., & Autistica. (2016). *Personal Tragedies, Public Crisis: The Urgent Need for a National Response to Early Death in Autism*. www.autistica.org.uk/downloads/files/Personal-tragedies-public-crisis-ONLINE.pdf

Summer, J., & Summer, J. (2024, March 22). *REM Sleep: What It Is and Why It's Important*. Sleep Foundation. www.sleepfoundation.org/stages-of-sleep/rem-sleep

Van Der Miesen, A.I.R., Hurley, H., Bal, A.M., and de Vries, A.L.C. (2018). Prevalence of the wish to be of the opposite gender in adolescents and adults with autism spectrum disorder. *Archives of Sexual Behavior*, 47(8), 2307–2317. doi:10.1007/s10508-018-1218-3.

Van Der Miesen, A.I.R., Hurley, H., & De Vries, A.L.C. (2016). Gender dysphoria and autism spectrum disorder: A narrative review. *International Review of Psychiatry*, 28(1), 70–80. https://doi.org/10.3109/09540261.2015.1111199

Warreman, E., Nooteboom, L., Terry, M., Hoek, H., Leenen, P., Van Rossum, E., Ramlal, D., Vermeiren, R., & Ester, W. (2023). Psychological, behavioural and biological factors associated with gastrointestinal symptoms in autistic adults and adults with autistic traits. *Autism*, 27(7), 2173–2186. https://doi.org/10.1177/13623613231155324

Wilkinson, L.A. (2017, March 1). Alexithymia, empathy, and autism. *Living Autism*. https://livingautism.com/alexithymia-empathy-autism

Chapter 6 – What Else Could It Be?

Aron, E. (1996). *The Highly Sensitive Person: How to Thrive When the World Overwhelms You.* Citadel.

Gilmore, R., Beezhold, J., Selwyn, V., Howard, R., Bartolome, I., Henderson, N. (2022). Is TikTok increasing the number of self-diagnoses of ADHD in young people? *European Psychiatry*, 65(S1), S571. doi:10.1192/j.eurpsy.2022.1463.

Chapter 7 – Screening Tests

Ratto, A.B., Bascom, J., da Vanport, S., Strang, J.F., et al. (2023). Centering the inner experience of autism: Development of the self-assessment of autistic traits. *Autism Adulthood*, 5(1), 93–105. doi:10.1089/aut.2021.0099. Erratum in: *Autism Adulthood*, 5(3), 344. doi:10.1089/aut.2021.0099.correx.

Chapter 9 – Self Diagnosis and Diagnostic Assessment

The Centers for Disease Control. (2023). *Autism Prevalence Higher, According to Data from 11 ADDM Communities.* www.cdc.gov/media/releases/2023/p0323-autism.html#

Lewis, L.F. (2016). Exploring the experience of self-diagnosis of autism spectrum disorder in adults. *Archives of Psychiatric Nursing*, 30(5), 575–580. doi:10.1016/j.apnu.2016.03.009.

Chapter 11 – It's a Yes, Now What?

Attwood, A., & Toudal, M. (2024). *Energy Accounting: Stress Management and Mental Health Monitoring for Autism and Related Conditions.* Jessica Kingsley Publishers.

Beardon, L. (2017). *Autism and Asperger Syndrome in Adults.* Sheldon Press.

Casanova, E.L., Baeza-Velasco, C., Buchanan, C.B., & Casanova, M.F. (2020). The relationship between autism and Ehlers-Danlos syndromes/hypermobility spectrum disorders. *Journal of Personalized Medicine*, 10(4), 260. https://doi.org/10.3390/jpm10040260

Jones, S. (2024). *The Autistic Survival Guide to Therapy*. Jessica Kingsley Publishers.

Maslow, A.H. (1943). A theory of human motivation. *Psychological Review*, 50, 370–396. http://dx.doi.org/10.1037/h0054346

Resources and Further Reading

We are aware that the majority of these resources are all in English and based in the UK and USA. Our apologies for this. The world is too big and this book too small to list resources in all countries. Hopefully, it will give you a start. Many books on autism and other neurodevelopmental conditions have been translated into other languages, so check out your local book retailers for those.

Chapters 1 and 2 – Autism Diagnosis and General Autism Information
Worldwide Autism Organizations
In Europe:

UK

National Institute for Clinical Excellence (NICE) guidelines, for diagnosis and management of autism – www.nice.org.uk/guidance/cg142

NHS England Right to Choose – www.nhs.uk/using-the-nhs/about-the-nhs/your-choices-in-the-nhs

National Autistic Society – www.autism.org.uk

Scottish Autism – www.scottishautism.org

SWAN (Scottish Women's Autism Network) – www.swanscotland.org

Autism Northern Ireland – www.autismni.org

Awtistiaeth Cymru/Autism Wales – autismwales.org/en

IRELAND

As I Am – www.asiam.ie

Irish Society Autism – www.autism.ie

ANDORRA

Associació d´Afectats d´Autisme d´Andorra (AUTEA) – www.autea.org/ca

GERMANY

Autismus Deutschland – www.autismus.de

HUNGARY

Hungarian Autistic Society – aosz.hu

FRANCE

Pro Aid Autisme – www.proaidautisme.com

Sesame Autisme – www.sesameautisme.fr

ITALY

Asperger Pride – aspergerpride.it

SPAIN

Autismo España – www.autismo.org.es

France, Italy, and Spain – each have their own guidelines which can be found on the Autism Europe website, although some of these also only focus on the diagnosis of children, but may give some insight as to what might be expected. www.autismeurope.org/about-autism/international-guidelines

NETHERLANDS

Nederlandse Vereniging voor Autisme – www.autisme.nl

FANN (Female Autism Network of the Netherlands) – www.fann-autisme.nl

PORTUGAL

Federaçao Portuguesa de Autismo – www.fpda.pt

DENMARK

Landsforeningen Autisme/Autism Denmark – www.autismeforening.dk

LUXEMBOURG

Foundation Autism Luxembourg – www.fal.lu

SWITZERLAND

Autisme Suisse – www.autismusschweiz.ch

ROMANIA

FEDRA – www.autismfedra.ro

In the rest of the world:

AUSTRALIA

Australia National Guideline for the Assessment and Diagnosis of ASD – www.autismcrc.com.au/best-practice/assessment-and-diagnosis

Autism Awareness Australia – www.autismawareness.com.au

Aspect – www.aspect.org.au

USA

The Centers for Disease Control Guidelines (no guidelines for the diagnosis of adults, only for children) – www.cdc.gov/ncbddd/autism/hcp-screening.html

AANE (American Association for Autism and Neurodiversity) – www.aane.org

CANADA

Autism Canada – www.autismcanada.org

Books on Autism

There are a huge number of books on all aspects of autism and autistic experience. Most can be found in major retailers online and increasingly in a number of languages. The main publishers for autism and neurodiversity books are Jessica Kingsley Publishers and Future Horizons, although there are several others. A number of these books can also be found as e-books or audio books.

Anderson, A. (2024). *This Is Who I Am: The Autistic Woman's Creative Guide to Belonging.* Jessica Kingsley Publishers.

Attwood, A., & Toudal, M. (2024). *Energy Accounting: Stress Management and Mental Health Monitoring for Autism and Related Conditions.* Jessica Kingsley Publishers.

Beardon, L. (2021). *Autism in Adults.* Sheldon Press.

Beardon, L. (2021). *Avoiding Anxiety in Adults.* Sheldon Press.

Beardon, L. (2023). *What Works for Autistic Adults.* Sheldon Press.

Garvey, N. (2023). *Looking After Your Autistic Self.* Jessica Kingsley Publishers.

Hendrickx, S. (2024). *Women and Girls on the Autistic Spectrum, 2nd edition.* Jessica Kingsley Publishers (translated into Polish, Spanish, Dutch, and Chinese).

Jones, S. (2024). *The Autistic Survival Guide to Therapy.* Jessica Kingsley Publishers.

Kotowicz, A. (2022). *What I Mean When I Say I'm Autistic.* Neurobeautiful.

Laine-Toner, K., & Payton, S. (2025). *Where Do I Start with Late Diagnosis Autism.* Jessica Kingsley Publishers.

Price, D. (2022). *Unmasking Autism.* Jessica Kingsley Publishers.

Silberman, S. (2015). *Neurotribes.* A&U.

Wylie, P. (2015). *Very Late Diagnosis of Asperger Syndrome (Autism Spectrum Disorder): How Seeking a Diagnosis in Adulthood Can Change Your Life.* Jessica Kingsley Publishers.

Social Media

There are a plethora of people on social media talking about their lived experiences. It can be overwhelming, but searching for #ActuallyAutistic might be a good place to start. Podcasts and videos can give a good insight into specific topics that you might want to learn more about and often this is the place that the autistic journey begins, when someone resonates strongly with a description of an autistic person's experience.

YOUTUBE

Purple Ella

Yo Samdy Sam

Orion Kelly – That Autistic Guy

Autism Explained

PODCASTS

The Squarepeg Podcast

Chapter 5 – Supporting Evidence

The following resources are ordered as they appear in Chapter 5.

Alexithymia

Autistica – Alexithymia Factsheet: www.autistica.org.uk/what-is-autism/anxiety-and-autism-hub/alexithymia

National Library of Medicine Research Article on Alexithymia: www.ncbi.nlm.nih.gov/pmc/articles/PMC8456171

Anxiety

MIND Mental Health – UK: www.mind.org.uk

Anxiety UK – UK: www.anxietyuk.org.uk

Mental Health America – USA: https://mhanational.org

Anxiety and Depression America – USA: https://adaa.org

Depression

MIND Mental Health – UK: www.mind.org.uk

Anxiety and Depression America – USA: https://adaa.org

Eating Differences/Disorders

Beat Eating Disorders Charity – UK: www.beateatingdisorders.org.uk

PEACE Pathway – UK: www.peacepathway.org

National Eating Disorders Association – USA: www.nationaleatingdisorders.org

Avoidant/Restrictive Food Intake Disorder (ARFID)

ARFID Awareness – UK: www.arfidawarenessuk.org

National Eating Disorders Association – USA: www.nationaleatingdisorders.org

Epilepsy

Epilepsy Research Institute – UK: https://epilepsy-institute.org.uk

Epilepsy Foundation – USA: www.epilepsy.com

Autistica – Managing Epilepsy in Autism: www.autistica.org.uk/downloads/files/Epilepsy-autism-E-LEAFLET.pdf

Myalgic Encephalomyelitis (ME)/ Chronic Fatigue Syndrome (CFS)

The ME Association – UK: https://meassociation.org.uk

The American ME and CFS Society: https://ammes.org

Fibromyalgia

The National Fibromyalgia Association – USA: www.fmaware.org

Fibromyalgia Action – UK: www.fmauk.org

Irritable Bowel Syndrome (IBS)

IBS Network – UK: www.theibsnetwork.org

American College of Gastroenterology – USA: https://gi.org/topics/irritable-bowel-syndrome

Food Intolerance

Allergy UK – UK: www.allergyuk.org

Food Allergy Research and Education – USA: www.foodallergy.org

Hypermobility/Ehlers Danlos Syndrome (EDS)

The Ehlers-Danlos Society: www.ehlers-danlos.com

Polycystic Ovary Syndrome (PCOS)

World Health Organization fact sheet: www.who.int/news-room/fact-sheets/detail/polycystic-ovary-syndrome

Premenstrual Dysphoric Disorder (PMDD)

International Association for Premenstrual Disorder: https://iapmd.org

Mind UK (mental health charity): www.mind.org.uk/information-support/types-of-mental-health-problems/premenstrual-dysphoric-disorder-pmdd/about-pmdd

ADHD

Additude – ADHD information resource: www.addnotudemag.com

ADHD UK Screening Test: https://adhduk.co.uk/adult-adhd-screening-survey

Dyslexia

British Dyslexia Association: www.bdadyslexia.org.uk

American Dyslexia Association: www.dyslexia.me

International Dyslexia Association Screening Test: https://dyslexiaida.org/dyslexia-test

Dyspraxia/DCD

Dyspraxia Foundation – UK: www.dyspraxiafoundation.org.uk

Dyspraxia Foundation – USA: https://dyspraxiausa.org

Dyspraxia DCD America – checklist: www.dyspraxiadcdamerica.org/dyspraxia-dcd-adults

Sleep Issues

The Sleep Charity – UK: https://thesleepcharity.org.uk

The National Sleep Foundation – USA: www.thensf.org

Neurodivergent Insights: https://neurodivergentinsights.com/autism-infographics/autism-and-sleep

Gender Identity

Gender Identity Research and Education Society – UK: www.gires.org.uk

Not A Phase – trans adult support – UK: https://notaphase.org

GLAAD – information and resources for LGBTQIA+ adults – USA: https://glaad.org

Chapter 6 – Alternative Explanations to Autism

These resources are presented in the order in which they appear in Chapter 6.

ADHD

Additude – ADHD information resource: www.additudemag.com

ADHD UK Screening Test: https://adhduk.co.uk/adult-adhd-screening-survey

Obsessive-Compulsive Disorder (OCD)

OCD Action – UK: https://ocdaction.org.uk

Internatioanal OCD Foundation: https://iocdf.org

Social Anxiety Disorder (SAD)

Social Anxiety Alliance – UK: https://socialanxietyalliance.org.uk

National Social Anxiety Center – USA: https://nationalsocialanxietycenter.com

Schizophrenia

Living with Schizophrenia – UK: https://livingwithschizophreniauk.org

Schizophrenia and Psychosis Action Alliance – USA: https://sczaction.org

Borderline Personality Disorder (BPD)/Emotionally Unstable Personality Disorder (EUPD)

BPD World – UK: www.bpdworld.org/about-us.html

National Education Alliance for Borderline Personality Disorder – USA: www.borderlinepersonalitydisorder.org

Post-Traumatic Stress Disorder (PTSD)/Complex Post-Traumatic Stress Disorder (C-PTSD)

PTSDUK – UK: www.ptsduk.org

National Center for PTSD – USA: www.ptsd.va.gov

Traumatic Brain Injury (TBI)

Headway – UK: www.headway.org.uk

Brain Injury Association of America – USA: www.biausa.org

Highly Sensitive Person (HSP)

Elaine Aron's website – author of HSP original book: https://hsperson.com

HSP Connect: https://hspconnect.uk

Attachment Disorder

Wikipedia description: https://en.wikipedia.org/wiki/Adult_attachment_disorder

Dyspraxia (DCD)

Dyspraxia Foundation – UK: www.dyspraxiafoundation.org.uk

Dyspraxia Foundation – USA: https://dyspraxiausa.org

Dyspraxia DCD America – checklist: www.dyspraxiadcdamerica.org/
dyspraxia-dcd-adults

Social Communication Disorder (SCD)

American Speech Language and Hearing Association: www.asha.org/
practice-portal/clinical-topics/social-communication-disorder

Sensory Processing Disorder (SPD)/
Sensory Integration Disorder (SID)

Spiral Foundation – USA: https://thespiralfoundation.org

Giftedness/Twice Exceptional

Intergifted – courses, assessments, coaching: https://intergifted.com

Chapter 7 – Screening Tests

These websites were all functioning at the time of publication. If they
no longer work, you can search for alternative sources. The tests are
ordered as they appear in Chapter 7.

Most of these tests, as well as a wealth of other information,
can be found at the excellent Embrace Autism website: https://
embrace-autism.com

Self-Assessment of Autistic Traits (SAAT): Research paper on development
of the test: www.ncbi.nlm.nih.gov/pmc/articles/PMC10024271

Autism Quotient (AQ50): https://embrace-autism.com/autism-spectrum-
quotient

Autism Quotient (AQ10): https://embrace-autism.com/aq-10

Camouflaging Autistic Traits Questionnaire (CAT-Q): https://embrace-
autism.com/cat-q

The Ritvo Autism Asperger Diagnostic Scale – Revised (RAADS-R): https://embrace-autism.com/raads-r

Aspie Quiz: https://embrace-autism.com/aspie-quiz

Repetitive Behaviours Questionnaire – version 2A (RBQ-2A): https://embrace-autism.com/rbq-2a

Empathy Quotient (EQ): https://embrace-autism.com/empathy-quotient

Systemizing Quotient (SQ): https://embrace-autism.com/systemizing-quotient-revised

Toronto Alexithymia Scale (TAS-20): https://embrace-autism.com/toronto-alexithymia-scale

Articles and Books Viewed but Not Referenced in the Text

Craig, F., Lamanna, A.L., Margari, F., Matera, E., Simone, M., & Margari, L. (2015). Overlap between autism spectrum disorders and attention deficit hyperactivity disorder: Searching for distinctive/common clinical features. *Autism Research*, 8(3), 328–337. https://doi.org/10.1002/aur.1449

Forde, J., Bonilla, P.M., Mannion, A., Coyne, R., Haverty, R., & Leader, G. (2021). Health status of adults with autism spectrum disorder. *Review Journal of Autism and Developmental Disorders*, 9(3), 427–437. https://doi.org/10.1007/s40489-021-00267-6

Fortuna, R.J., Robinson, L., Smith, T.H., Meccarello, J., Bullen, B., Nobis, K., & Davidson, P.W. (2015). Health conditions and functional status in adults with autism: A cross-sectional evaluation. *Journal of General Internal Medicine*, 31(1), 77–84. https://doi.org/10.1007/s11606-015-3509-x

Hartman, D., Kavanagh, M., Azevedo, J., O'Donnell-Killen, T., Doyle, J., & Day, A. (2023). *The Adult Autism Assessment Handbook: A Neurodiversity Affirmative Approach*. Jessica Kingsley Publishers.

Hours, C., Recasens, C., & Baleyte, J.M. (2022). ASD and ADHD comorbidity: What are we talking about? *Frontiers in Psychiatry*, 13, 837424. https://doi.org/10.3389/fpsyt.2022.837424

Kinnaird, E., Stewart, C., & Tchanturia, K. (2019). Investigating alexithymia in autism: A systematic review and meta-analysis. *European Psychiatry*, 55, 80–89. https://doi.org/10.1016/j.eurpsy.2018.09.004

Kosidou, K., Dalman, C., Widman, L., Arver, S., Lee, B.K., Magnusson, C., & Gardner, R.M. (2015). Maternal polycystic ovary syndrome and the risk of autism spectrum disorders in the offspring: A population-based nation-wide study in Sweden. *Molecular Psychiatry*, 21(10), 1441–1448. https://doi.org/10.1038/mp.2015.183

National Autistic Society. (n.d.). *Epilepsy and Autism*. www.autism.org.uk/advice-and-guidance/professional-practice/epilepsy-autism

National Autistic Society. (n.d.). *Synaesthesia in Autism*. www.autism.org.uk/advice-and-guidance/professional-practice/synaesthesia

Taniya, M.A., Chung, H., Mamun, A.A., Alam, S., Aziz, M.A., Emon, N.U., Islam, M.M., Hong, S.S., Podder, B.R., Mimi, A.A., Suchi, S.A., & Xiao, J. (2022). Role of gut microbiome in autism spectrum disorder and its thera-peutic regulation. *Frontiers in Cellular and Infection Microbiology*, 12. https://doi.org/10.3389/fcimb.2022.915701

Weir, E., Allison, C., & Baron-Cohen, S. (2021). Understanding the substance use of autistic adolescents and adults: A mixed-methods approach. *The Lancet: Psychiatry*, 8(8), 673–685. https://doi.org/10.1016/s2215-0366(21)00160-7

Appendix

Notes and Thoughts Pages

A key part of the criteria of autism is that any differences must have been present from childhood. When taking notes, consider how you have navigated the world and any difficulties you have had since childhood, through your teen years, and into adulthood. Think of examples of strategies that you may have implemented over the years and what would happen if those were taken away from you or you were unable to do them.

Think about family members who may display these features, even though they have not been diagnosed. This can add weight to your evidence.

Ask family members for input if you have told them you are exploring the idea you might be autistic. They may have useful insights and examples.

As well as gathering your thoughts towards making a decision about whether autism is a good fit for your thought processes and experiences, these notes may be extremely useful if you decide to seek formal assessment, as they can form the basis of any questionnaire that you are asked to complete, and also help when you are asked questions during an assessment interview.

Chapter 1 and 2 Diagnostic Criteria
Communication and Language

Age you started to speak (any delays/difficulties/advancements/support):

. . . .

. . . .

In both adulthood and childhood, consider:

- Talking too much/too little, knowing when to speak
- Small talk ability/enjoyment
- Bluntness/perceived social errors
- Recognizing non-verbal cues – facial expressions, body language, tone of voice
- Own facial expressions and tone of voice
- Correcting errors made by others/recognizing social hierarchies
- Understanding language in a literal and/or precise way
- Understanding sarcasm and humour
- Recognizing hidden agendas and lies/being naive and easily tricked

- . . . .

- . . . .

- . . . .

- . . . .

- . . . .

- . . . .

- . . . .

- . . . .

- . . . .

Social Interaction

In both adulthood and childhood, consider:

- Eye contact
- Friendships/relationships – many/few/online/selective/ passive/dominant
- Bullied or bullying others, unhealthy/abusive relationships, vulnerability to predators
- Social situations – enjoyment/seek/avoid/own performance
- Capacity for socializing length or frequency
- Observing/masking/mimicking
- Giving emotional support to others

- . . . .
- . . . .
- . . . .
- . . . .
- . . . .
- . . . .
- . . . .
- . . . .
- . . . .

Flexibility of Thought

In both adulthood and childhood, consider:

- Routines, sequencing, and order in daily life
- Need for schedules and plans
- Change, interruptions, spontaneity, and surprises
- Black-and-white thinking style – binary, right/wrong, yes/no
- Focus on small details and miss context, or see the bigger picture

- Analytical and logical thinking style
- Data, facts, research
- Pattern, change, and error spotting
- Repetition and sameness of activities, purchases, foods
- Placement of items, symmetry
- Decision making

- ....
- ....
- ....
- ....
- ....
- ....
- ....
- ....
- ....
- ....

Interests

Interests in childhood and adulthood that were/are intense, deep, and all-consuming in nature:

- Expert knowledge gained – may form basis for career
- Retention of large amount of facts
- Tendency to monologue, and switch conversation to or think constantly about topic

- ....
- ....
- ....
- ....

- ....
- ....
- ....
- ....
- ....

Sensory Preferences

Sensory stimuli that are sought or avoided both in childhood and adulthood:

- Noise
- Food – taste, texture, sameness, limited choices, brands
- Touch – clothing and people
- Smells
- Light
- Features of synaesthesia
- Interoception difficulties – recognizing hunger, thirst, or needing the bathroom

- ....
- ....
- ....
- ....
- ....
- ....
- ....
- ....
- ....
- ....

Repetitive Movements

- Repetitive movements which may include, flapping, skin picking, spinning, rocking, tapping

- . . . .
- . . . .
- . . . .

Early Development

- Developmental delays or advancements
- Treatments or interventions

- . . . .
- . . . .
- . . . .
- . . . .

Childhood Play

- Alone/with peers
- Passive/dominant
- Preferred activities
- Repetition in play
- Lining up, sorting, ordering, scene setting, dressing/undressing
- Original narrative play, repeating seen/heard scenarios

- . . . .
- . . . .
- . . . .
- . . . .
- . . . .

- ....
- ....
- ....
- ....

Anything else you feel is relevant:

....
....
....
....
....
....
....
....

Chapter 3 – Reasons for Considering Autism

Why are you seeking an assessment now?

....
....
....
....
....
....
....
....

Chapter 4 – Reasons I Can't Be Autistic

Reasons I can't be autistic:

. . . .

. . . .

. . . .

. . . .

. . . .

. . . .

. . . .

. . . .

Chapter 5 – Supporting Evidence:

Note date and age of diagnosis:

. . . .

. . . .

- Alexithymia
- Anxiety
- Depression
- Eating differences/disorders
- Epilepsy
- Chronic fatigue/ME
- Fibromyalgia
- IBS
- Food intolerances
- Hypermobility/EDS
- PCOS
- PMDD
- ADHD
- Dyslexia

- Dyspraxia/DCD
- Sleep issues
- Gender identity/sexuality

Family History
Suspected or diagnosed conditions in biological family members:

....

....

....

....

....

....

....

....

Chapter 6 – Alternative Explanations
Other possible explanations that fit more closely with your profile than autism – note supporting reasons for any that apply.

- Attachment disorder
- Borderline personality disorder (BPD)/emotionally unstable personality disorder (EUPD)
- Dyspraxia (DCD)
- Highly sensitive person (HSP)
- Social communication disorder (SCD)
- Obsessive-compulsive disorder (OCD)
- Schizophrenia
- Sensory processing disorder (SPD)/Sensory integration disorder (SID)
- Social anxiety disorder (SAD)
- Traumatic brain injury (TBI)

- Post-traumatic stress disorder (PTSD)/complex post-trau-matic stress disorder (C-PTSD)
- Giftedness
- Twice exceptional

- ....
- ....
- ....
- ....
- ....
- ....
- ....
- ....
- ....
- ....

Chapter 7 – Screening Tests

Scores of online tests:

- AQ-50: ....
- AQ-10: ....
- CAT-Q: ....
- RAADS-R: ....
- The Aspie Quiz: ....
- RBQ-2A: ....
- SQ: ....
- EQ: ....

- Other: ....

- ....

- ....

- ....

- ....

Other Notes and Thoughts

....

....

....

....

....

....

....

....

....

....

....

....

....

....

....

....

Subject Index

Author Index